MW01005984

the singular objects of architecture

University of Minnesota Press Minneapolis — London

thee s isingular r o lobjects o fof r c la'rchitecture

Jean **Baudrillard** and Jean **Nouvel**

translated by Robert Bononno **foreword by** K. Michael Hays

The University of Minnesota Press gratefully acknowledges translation assistance provided for this book by the French Ministry of Culture.

The publication of this book was assisted by a bequest from Josiah H. Chase to honor his parents, Ellen Rankin Chase and Josiah Hook Chase, Minnesota territorial pioneers.

Originally published in French as *Les objets singuliers: Architecture et philosophie*, by Jean Baudrillard and Jean Nouvel. Copyright 2000 by Editions Calmann-Lévy.

English translation copyright 2002 by Robert Bononno

Published by the University of Minnesota Press
111 Third Avenue South, Suite 290
Minneapolis, MN 55401-2520
http://www.upress.umn.edu

Library of Congress Cataloging-in-Publication Data

Baudrillard, Jean.
    [Objets singuliers. English]
    The singular objects of architecture / Jean Baudrillard and Jean
  Nouvel ; translated by Robert Bononno.
      p.   cm.
    ISBN 0-8166-3912-4 (alk. paper)
    1. Architecture—Philosophy.   2. Aesthetics.   I. Nouvel,
Jean, 1945-   II. Title.
    NA2500.B3413 2002
    720'.1—dc21

                           2002008024

Printed in the United States of America on acid-free paper

The University of Minnesota is an equal-opportunity educator and employer.

12 11 10 09 08 07 06 05 04 03 02   10 9 8 7 6 5 4 3 2 1

Contents

Foreword

K. Michael Hays

The Singular Objects of Architecture should not create the expectation that either architecture or philosophy will be treated in this dialogue in anything like a traditional way (which, were it the case, would seem not so much old-fashioned as reactionary, coming from two of the few cultural figures practicing today that we could still dare to call progressive). Indeed, it is better to state the reverse: what first strikes one as extraordinary about this conversation is that architecture and philosophy are treated with any distinction at all by progressive thinkers in our present era. In our own time, the de-differentiation of disciplines and the tendentious erasure of boundaries between specific cultural materials and practices promise to homogenize all distinction, difference, and otherness into a globalized, neutralized sameness. Much of what claims to be progressive thought is happy to aestheticize this situation, to accelerate its effects, and to trade in any remaining individuality or singularity of thought for a randomized, spread-out delirium. The flattening seems to have been chosen. Besides, any disciplinary autonomy or expertise that might counter this leveling tendency is destined to be crushed anyway under the massive movement of the world system itself, to be emulsified along with everything else into so many cultural and economic fluids. What is extraordinary about this conversation, then, is its declaration, against all that, to search for singular objects (rather than globalized fluids) as might be found in architecture and philosophy.

"We're not heading for disaster, we're already in the midst of total disaster," Nouvel declares at one point. Yet neither he nor Baudrillard ever laments the loss of a real or idealized past, nor do they accept, not even for a moment, the cynically complacent preemption of the future. The second surprise of *The Singular Objects of Architecture* is that what is offered, both as program and as practice exemplified in this particular dialogue, is a renewal of utopian thought, a revived attempt at envisioning a possible future out of our disastrous present, a way of thinking that has been under ban now for more than two decades. Against the hegemony of the antiutopian, real-time thinking of our contemporary technocratic positivism and experiential nominalism ("What's mine is mine, and you can't feel it"), the singular object must be anticipatory, inexhaustible, and shared; it must destroy culture (or what has become of it) and redistribute the leftovers. And so, while architecture and philosophy are treated together as parts of a period problem—as disciplines and practices with specific histories, transitions, and transformations, subjected to the desultory effects of history now, in our own period—they will not remain unchallenged or unchanged in this dialogue. If the singular object is to be both utopian and destructive, future directed and exquisitely representative of the present, it will be a peculiar object indeed. Its model will be neither architecture nor philosophy freestanding, as traditionally practiced, but a productive enfolding of one into the other—an event more than an object, a constructional operation in which each discourse interprets the other but nevertheless produces a new, irreducible, singular thing: that peculiar thing we call theory. "I feel that thought, theory, is inexchangeable," says Baudrillard. "It can't be exchanged for truth or for reality. Exchange is impossible. It's because of this that theory even exists." Theory is the diagram of the singular object of architecture. This, at least, should come as no surprise, for work of such large ambition as is evidenced here is to be found today almost nowhere other than theory.

Theory is ready to travel. Although at its best, theory will stay close to the historicity of its material, mediating between specific cultural practices and specific historical contexts, theoretical constructions also possess an uncanny capacity to cross over, drift, and expand across disciplines, however much authors, institutions, and orthodoxies try to confine them. Theory is autonomous ("inexchangeable"), but it is nourished by circulation—by borrowing and trading, by unconscious influence or wholesale appropriation. Through the accidents of discourse, a body of theory can also be dislodged and pressed into the service of a quite different one, reinvested with unpredicted content, and refunctioned for unexpected vocations.

Not least among such transactions is that between architecture and philosophy, provided we understand that coupling in an expanded sense to include urbanism, semiology, *Ideologiekritik,* and certain strains of poststructuralist thought; for it is that fusion (what we now call, simply, architecture theory) that, since the mid-1960s, has so energized architectural discourse in academic and professional circles, turning us away from an earlier functionalist, empiricist, foundationalist way of thinking and toward new registers of signification. By the 1980s, architecture theory had discovered affinities with other branches of theory and developed concerns with textual strategies, constructions of subjectivity and gender, power and property, geopolitics, and other themes that were already part of the general poststructuralist repertoire but whose spatial dimension was now foregrounded. This entailed that the emphasis on the production of architectural objects (which aimed to prescribe normative standards for design and layout methods and motives for implementation) should give way to an emphasis on the production of architecture as a subject of knowledge. Theory took on the task of revealing the unintended ideological presumptions that architectural procedures and techniques alternately enabled or tried to remove from the possibility of thinking, which is to say that theory understood architecture as one of culture's primary representational systems.

The concern with the specific internal workings of architecture—which tend to be mainly synchronic, synthetic, and projective—was not abandoned so much as folded into various discourses of context and exteriority, recalibrated according to what was sayable or thinkable in the idiolects of Marxism, deconstruction, psychoanalysis, and other imported systems. But these systems were not merely yoked together with architecture. Rather, something of a shift of level, as much as perspective, took place, in which architecture's specific forms, operations, and practices could now more clearly be seen as producing concepts whose ultimate horizon of effect lay outside architecture "proper," in a more general sociocultural field. This new activity of theory demanded not new ideas for buildings but the invention of altogether new techniques for rethinking issues of representation, foundation, subjectivity, structure and ornament, materiality, media, and more. What used to be called philosophy, then, began to think its problems *through architecture* rather than the other way around. And this inevitably attracted some of the most important thinkers of our time (including Roland Barthes, Michel Foucault, Jacques Derrida, and Fredric Jameson) to ponder architectural problems.

There has rarely been a sustained conversation between a philosopher and an architect of the scope and focus that we have here. Then again, a certain horizontality of thought, along with the desire to interpret the totality, seems demanded by our current situation. For all the apparently wild multiplicity of our present system of objects, there is also the constant magnetic pull of the single global market and a corporate-controlled retotalization of all the dispersed vocations and functions of social life into a single space-time of consumption and communication. Our different day-to-day activities are no longer tied to determinate needs or to specific exchanges between people and objects, but rather to a total universe of signs and simulacra floating in economic and cultural-informational fluids. Even the conscious ideologies of rebellion and negative critique seem to be not so much co-opted by the system as a strategic part of the system's internal workings. At certain moments, in certain singular objects, architecture itself produces the perception of this conflictedly overdetermined situation; architecture becomes a kind of precipitate of the vapor that we used to call the social. The twinness of the World Trade Center, for example—a building that was a replica of itself—was already, in the 1960s when the towers were built, an anticipatory sign of the computerized, genetically networked, cloning society that was emerging. In the next decade, the Centre Pompidou, even more deeply conflicted, signals the catastrophic finishing off of mass culture by the masses themselves: a new breed of cultural consumer who is also, along with the paintings and the cash, both the raw material and the product of the new museum. And then the architecture of our own time (the Guggenheim Museum Bilbao, perhaps, one of infinite possible clones or chimeras spun out of a software package) seems to become altogether virtual, for an audience that is everyone and everywhere—not so much an architectural readymade (in the sense of Duchamp) as an architecture already made, a transparent cutout that is its own template.

In their conversation, Baudrillard and Nouvel turn over and over again possible ways of understanding this situation and its agents, mapping it through the languages of architecture, philosophy, and both together (and it is fascinating to register the slippages of perspective between the architect and the philosopher, to compare how the mind feels performing work on the problem one way and then the other, but also to become aware of the preference that both have for a description of the totality over the separate, abstract parts). But the provocations, responses, and probes are not meant to *préciser* the ways in which architecture simply replicates the base-and-superstructure apparatus of which it is a primary organ (the code words for such ideological reproduction include "screen architecture" and "clone architecture," but also the neutral and the global). Baudrillard and Nouvel search also for some autonomous force or effect produced by the object not *in* culture but alongside it, in the penumbra of culture, a force that thickens the situation, obscures the scene, and gums up the hegemonic workings of visibility and transparency. This attribute of the object is alternately called its "secret," its "radicality," its "literality," or indeed its singularity. But clearly this is an apprehension of the singular object quite the reverse of any that would fixate on aesthetic properties to the exclusion of larger, "extrinsic" factors. Rather, the singular object is the way of access, through the coils of contradiction, to be sure, but nevertheless opening onto the determining conditions of its own cultural surround.

Take Nouvel's own work, which has famously found its identity in a logic of the surface. On the one hand, from the earliest stone facades to the steel and glass curtain wall, architecture has always played a game of contradiction with mass and gravity and their dematerialization into surface. On the other hand, from our present perspective, the logic of the surface is a perceptual logic we must now understand as having been given to us by consumer-communication culture and its slick advertising two-dimensionality. "Screen architecture"? "Clone architecture"? Or singular object. It is the particular handling of the surface that must make a difference. As Nouvel has commented on his Cartier Foundation: "If I look at the facade, since it's bigger than the building, I can't tell if I'm looking at the reflection of the sky or at the sky through the glass. . . . If I look at a tree through the three glass panes, I can never determine if I'm looking at the tree through the glass, in front of it, behind it, or the reflection of the tree. And when I plant two trees in parallel, even accidentally, to the glass plane, I can't tell if there's a second tree or if it's a real tree."

For Baudrillard, this form of illusion is not gratuitous; in his essay "Truth or Radicality in Architecture," he referred to it as a "dramaturgy of illusion and seduction." Such destabilizations of perception thwart the dictatorship of the smoothly visible and install an alternative perception, a "secret image," an almost bodily recalcitrance (Barthes's punctum is mentioned as a model), which will make itself felt as a kind of resistance, lag, or refraction beneath the transparency. An object both of a culture and the culture's biggest threat, then: pained by the loss, anticipating the gain, a representation of the moment and a momentary refusal.

The singular object is deeply conflicted, and the conversation here takes on its subject's form. We can't go on; we must go on. The architect stretching to imagine what it would take to actually make a singular object, the philosopher insisting that no intention, no amount of individual effort, can guarantee singularity's arrival ("let's not think too much"). Both against premature clarification: I know it's here, but I can't see it; "the important thing is to have looked." Rarely can so many conflicting things be said about a singular subject. Rarely has such conflict been so productive.

Acknowledgments

The authors would like to thank the Maison des Écrivains and the University of Paris VI–La Villette School of Architecture for taking the initiative to sponsor a conference between architects and philosophers. The project, titled *Urban Passages,* involved a series of six encounters between writers and architects in 1997 and 1998, which made headlines both inside and outside the school. The extended dialogue between Jean Baudrillard and Jean Nouvel forms the basis of the present text. The five other pairs of participants were Paul Chemetov and Didier Daeninckx, Henri Gaudin and Jean-Pierre Vernant, Philippe Sollers and Christian de Portzamparc, Antoine Grumbach and Antoine Bailly, and Henri Ciriani and Olivier Rolin. Hélène Bleskine developed the idea for *Urban Passages* and organized the dialogues. We are grateful for the opportunity to hold discussions of such quality, since it is through speech that we communicate to others the singularity of an encounter.

When it came time to publish the book, the authors reworked their dialogue, focusing on a recurrent theme of the discussions: singularity. This theme helped drive the discussions toward their resolution or, we should say, toward their radical and necessary incompletion.

I
First Interview

Radicality

Jean Baudrillard: We can't begin with nothing because, logically, nothingness is the culmination of something. When I think of radicality, I think of it more in terms of writing and theory than of architecture. I am more interested in the radicality of space. . . . But it's possible that true radicality is the radicality of nothingness. Is there a radical space that is also a void? The question interests me because now, at last, I have an opportunity to gain insight into how we can fill a space, how we can organize it by focusing on something other than its radical extension—vertically or horizontally, that is—within a dimension where anything is possible. Yet we still need to produce something real. . . . The question I want to ask Jean Nouvel, since we have to start somewhere, is very simple: "Is there such a thing as architectural truth?"

Jean Nouvel: What do you mean by "truth"?

J.B. Architectural truth isn't a truth or a reality in the sense that architecture might exhaust itself in its references, its finalities, its destination, its modes, its procedures. Doesn't architecture transcend all of that, effectively exhausting itself in something else, its true finality, or something that would enable it to go beyond its true finality. . . . Does architecture exist beyond this limit of the real?

Singular Objects in Architecture

J.B. I've never been interested in architecture. I have no specific feelings about it one way or the other. I'm interested in space, yes, and in anything in so-called "constructed" objects that enables me to experience the instability of space. I'm most interested in buildings like Beaubourg, the World Trade Center, Biosphere 2—singular objects, but objects that aren't exactly architectural wonders as far as I'm concerned. It's not the architectural sense of these buildings that captivates me but the world they translate. If I examine the truth of the twin towers of the World Trade Center, for example, I see that, in that location, architecture expresses, signifies, translates a kind of full, constructed form, the context of a society already experiencing hyperrealism. Those two towers resemble two perforated bands. Today we'd probably say they're clones of each other, that they've already been cloned. Did they anticipate our present? Does that mean that architecture is not part of reality but part of the fiction of a society, an anticipatory illusion? Or does architecture simply translate what is already there? That's why I asked, "Is there such a thing as architectural truth?" in the sense that there would be a suprasensible destination for architecture and for space.

J.N. Before answering your question, I would just like to comment that this dialogue provides a unique opportunity to discuss architecture in other than the customary terms. You know that I consider you to be the one intellectual who is actually doing his job. You respond to the many disturbing questions, the real questions, with questions and answers that no one wants to hear. I don't know if I'll be able to provoke any responses in a field that you claim to be unfamiliar with, that doesn't really interest you, but this evening I'm going to try. Recently I had a look at some of your books, and I was pleased to find that you never speak about architecture except in an interview that took place twelve years ago between us. It's in that interview that I discovered a number of your ideas about architecture, aside from your writing on New York or Beaubourg. I took notes on some of your thoughts about our architectural monstrosities and some of your more radical points of view, which could supply us with a number of questions.

If we attempt to talk about architecture as a limit—and that's what really interests me—we do so by always positioning ourselves on the fringe of knowledge and ignorance. That's the true adventure of architecture. And that adventure is situated in a real world, a world that implies a consensus. You said, somewhere, that a consensus must exist in order for seduction to occur. Now, the field of architecture is a field that, by the very nature of things, revolves around a world of seduction. The architect is in a unique situation. He's not an artist in the traditional sense. He's not someone who meditates in front of a blank page. He doesn't work on a canvas. I often compare the architect to the film director, because we have roughly the same limitations. We're in a situation where we have to produce an object within a given period of time, with a given budget, for a specific group of individuals. And we work as a team. We're in a situation where we can be censored, directly or indirectly, for reasons of safety or money, or even because of deliberate censorship. It's a field where there are professional censors. We could even call an architect who designs buildings in France a "French building censor." It's exactly the same thing. We are situated in an environment that is bound, limited. Within that environment, where can we find an unrestricted space and the means to overcome those limitations?

In my case, I've looked for it in the articulation of various things, especially the formulation of a certain way of thinking. So should I use the word "concept" or not? I used it very early on, realizing that the word is philosophically appropriate. Then we may want to introduce the terms "percept" and "affect," in reference to Deleuze, but that's not the real problem. The problem lies in our ability to articulate a project around a preliminary concept or idea, using a very specific strategy that can synergize—or sometimes even juxtapose—perceptions that will interact with one another and define a place we are unfamiliar with. We are still dealing with invention, the unknown, risk. This unfamiliar place, if we succeed in figuring out what's going on, could be the locus of a secret. And it might, assuming that's the case, then convey certain things, things we cannot control, things that are fatal, voluntarily uncontrolled. We need to find a compromise between what we control and what we provoke. All the buildings I've tried to build until now are based on the articulation of these three things. They also refer to a concept that I know interests you, the concept of illusion.

Illusion, Virtuality, Reality

J.N. I'm no magician, but I try to create a space that isn't legible, a space that works as the mental extension of sight. This seductive space, this virtual space of illusion, is based on very precise strategies, strategies that are often diversionary. I frequently use what I find around me, including your own work and that of a few others. I also make use of cinema. So when I say that I play with depth of field, it's because I'm trying to foreground a series of filters that could lead anywhere—a kind of metanarrative—but from that point on, the intellect goes into action. This is not entirely my invention. Look at the Japanese garden. There is always a vanishing point, the point at which we don't know whether the garden stops or continues. I'm trying to provoke that sort of response.

If we look at the phenomenon of perspective—I'm thinking of the project for superimposing a grid on the horizon, which I had prepared for La Tête Défense—I was attempting to step outside Alberti's logic. In other words, I was trying to organize all the elements in such a way that they could be read in series and, if need be, to play with scale using the series' rhythm, so the viewer would become conscious of the space. What happens if I escape those limits? What if I say that the building isn't between the horizon and the observer but is part of that horizon? Assuming this, what happens if it loses its materiality?

Dematerialization is something that would interest you; the "endless skyscraper" is one example. [Nouvel's project for a *Tour sans fin*, or "endless skyscraper," was designed for La Défense, just outside central Paris. Although his design won an international competition, the building was never constructed.] Again, this isn't something I invented. I think Deleuze, in *Proust and Signs*, spoke about it from a different point of view. This diversion, which reroutes our perception of phenomena from the material to the immaterial, is a concept that architecture should appropriate for itself. Using these kinds of concepts, we can create more than what we see. And this "more than what we see" is manifest in and through physical context. With respect to what architecture has borrowed from cinema, the concept of sequence is very important, as Paul Virilio reminds us. In other words, concepts such as displacement, speed, memory seen in terms of an imposed trajectory, or a known trajectory, enable us to compose an architectural space based not only on what we see but on what we have memorized as a succession of sequences that are perceived to follow one another. From this point on, there are contrasts between what is created and what was originally present in our perception of space.

In the Versailles Theater, you enter through a stone corridor, which is absolutely neutral, plain, devoid of decoration, and which opens suddenly into something absolutely stunning in terms of its decoration, its preciosity. The period in which this theater was designed, imagined, realized provides us with a key to the phenomenon I have been describing. We're no longer in the same place today, however. We need to put those ideas aside and make use of others—ideas like contrast, chaining, and extension—to serve as fundamental concepts of the architectural project. At the same time, when I play with the concept of a virtual space, in the magician's sense, it's because space and architecture are things we become conscious of through our eyes. So we can play with anything the eye can integrate through sight, and we can fool the eye. Classical culture has often made use of this kind of sleight of hand. In a building like the Cartier Foundation, where I intentionally blend the real image and the virtual image, it signifies that within a given plane, I no longer know if I'm looking at the virtual image or the real image. If I look at the facade, since it's bigger than the building, I can't tell if I'm looking at the reflection of the sky or the sky through the glass. . . . If I look at a tree through the three glass planes, I can never determine if I'm looking at the tree through the glass, in front of it, behind it, or the reflection of the tree. And when I plant two trees in parallel, even accidentally, to the glass plane, I can't tell if there's a second tree or if it's a real tree. These are gimmicks, things we can put into our bag of tricks, our architectural bag of tricks, and which we're never supposed to talk about, but which, from time to time, must be talked about. These are the means by which architecture creates a virtual space or a mental space; it's a way of tricking the senses. But it's primarily a way of preserving a destabilized area.

A Destabilized Area?

J.N. When you talk to a developer, the way a director talks to a producer, he asks a ton of questions about the price per square meter, the lot, can it be built on, will it shock the local bourgeoisie, a whole series of questions of this type. And then there are those things that remain unsaid. There is always something unsaid; that's part of the game. And what remains unsaid is, ethically, something additional, something that doesn't run counter to what is being sold or exchanged, doesn't interfere with our notions of economics, but signifies something vital. That's where the game is played. Because if an architectural object is only the translation of some functionality, if it's only the result of an economic situation, it can't have meaning. What's more, there's a passage in one of your texts on New York that I like very much, where you say that the city embodies a form of architecture that is violent, brutal, immediate, which is the true form of architecture, that you have no need for eco-architecture or genteel architecture because that would impede life's energy. What I'm saying doesn't necessarily contradict that. But since we're not always in New York, we need to set aside places, areas that can be destabilized.

J.B. I agree, except perhaps about terms like "consensus." . . . When you say that seduction is consensual, I'm skeptical.

J.N. You mean only with reference to architecture?

J.B. Precisely. It's a way of confronting it through the visible and the invisible. I don't talk much about architecture, but in all my books, the question lies just beneath the surface. . . . I fully agree with this idea of invisibility. What I like very much in your work is that we don't see it, things remain invisible, they know how to make themselves invisible. When you stand in front of the buildings, you see them, but they're invisible to the extent that they effectively counteract that hegemonic visibility, the visibility that dominates us, the visibility of the system, where everything must be immediately visible and immediately interpretable. You conceive space in such a way that architecture simultaneously creates both place and nonplace, is also a nonplace in this sense, and thus creates a kind of apparition. And it's a seductive space. So I take back what I said earlier: Seduction isn't consensual. It's dual. It must confront an object with the order of the real, the visible order that surrounds it. If this duality doesn't exist—if there's no interactivity, no context—seduction doesn't take place. A successful object, in the sense that it exists outside its own reality, is an object that creates a dualistic relation, a relation that can emerge through diversion, contradiction, destabilization, but which effectively brings the so-called reality of a world and its radical illusion face-to-face.

Concept, Irresolution, Vertigo

J.B. Let's talk about radicality. Let's talk about the kind of radical exoticism of things that Ségalen discusses, the estrangement from a sense of identity that results in the creation of a form of vertigo through which all sorts of things can occur: affects, concepts, prospects, whatever, but always something insoluble, something unresolved. In this sense, yes, architectural objects, or at least yours or others that are even more undomesticated, are part of an architecture without a referent. This reflects their quality of being "unidentified," and ultimately unidentifiable, objects. This is one area where we can combine—and not merely by deliberate analogy—writing, fiction, architecture, and a number of other things as well, obviously, whether this involves the analysis of a society, an event, or an urban context. I agree that we can't choose the event, we can only choose the concept, but we retain the right to make this choice. The choice of a concept is something that should conflict with the context, with all the significations (positive, functional, etc.) a building can assume, or a theory, or anything else.

Deleuze defined the concept as something antagonistic. However, with respect to the event, as it is given, as it is seen, as it is deciphered, overdetermined by the media or other voices, by information, the concept is that which creates the nonevent. It creates an event to the extent that it juxtaposes the so-called "real" event with a theoretical or fictional nonevent of some sort. I can see how this can happen with writing, but I have a much harder time with architecture. In your work, I feel it in the effect produced by this illusion you spoke of earlier; not in the sense of an illusion or a trompe l'oeil—well, ultimately, yes, of course, but not an illusion in the sense of a simulation—of something that takes place beyond the reflection of things or beyond the screen. Today we are surrounded by screens. In fact, it's rare to succeed in creating a surface or place that doesn't serve as a screen and can exert all the prestige of transparency without the dictatorship.

I'd like to make a distinction here regarding our terminology. Illusion is not the same as the virtual, which, in my opinion, is complicit with hyperreality, that is, the visibility of an imposed transparency, the space of the screen, mental space, and so on. Illusion serves as a sign for anything else. It seems to me that everything you do, and do well, is another architecture seen through a screen. Precisely because to create something like an inverse universe, you must completely destroy that sense of fullness, that sense of ripe visibility, that oversignification we impose on things.

And here I'd like to know, as part of this question of context, what happens to social and political data, to everything that can constrain things, when architecture is tempted to become the expression, or even the sociological or political transformer, of a social reality, which is an illusion—in the negative sense of the term. In one sense, even if architecture wants to respond to a political program or fulfill social needs, it will never succeed because it is confronted, fortunately, by something that is also a black hole. And this black hole simply means that the "masses" are still there and they are not at all recipients, or conscious, or reflected, or anything; it's an extremely perverse operator with respect to everything that is constructed. So even if architecture wants what it wants and tries to signify what it wants to express, it will be deflected. You, however, strive for this deflection and destabilization, and you're right. And as we discussed, it's going to happen anyway. This is true of politics; it's true of other categories as well. Something is present, but that something is nothing; there's nothing on the other side. Because where we see plenitude, masses, populations, statistics, and so on, there's always deflection. It's this deflection of the operator, for example, that in a work of architecture or art transforms the way we use it, but also, ultimately, transforms the meaning that was originally given to the work. And whether this resides in the work of art or in something else, at any given moment the singular object is rendered enigmatic, unintelligible even to the one who created it, which obsesses and delights us.

Fortunately, this is also the reason why we can continue to live in a universe that is as full, as determined, as functional as this. Our world would be unlivable without this power of innate deflection, and this has nothing to do with sociology. On the contrary, sociology records and tallies up official behaviors before it transforms them into statistics. I'm relativizing the architectural object somewhat, even though I'm fully aware that when we create something, we have to want it in some sense by saying to ourselves that even if there is no reality principle or truth principle for those for whom the object is intended, there will be a fatal deflection, there will be seduction. And we have to make sure that the things that assume they are identical to themselves or people who think they are identifying with their own character, their own genius, will be deflected, destabilized, seduced. In my opinion, seduction always takes place in this sense, in its most general form. However, I'm not sure that in the virtualized world of new technologies, information, and the media, this dualistic, indecipherable relationship of seduction will take place as it did before. It's possible that the secret you spoke about would be completely annihilated by another type of universe. It's also possible that in this universe of the virtual, which we talk about today, architecture wouldn't exist at all, that this symbolic form, which plays with weight, the gravity of things and their absence, their total transparence, would be abolished. No, I'm no longer sure this could occur in the virtual universe. We are completely screened in; the problem of architecture is expressed differently. So maybe there's a kind of completely superficial architecture that is confused with this universe. This would be an architecture of banality, of virtuality. It can be original as well, but it wouldn't be part of the same concept.

Creation and Forgetfulness

J.N. One of the big problems with architecture is that it must both exist and be quickly forgotten; that is, lived spaces are not designed to be experienced continuously. The architect's problem is that he is always in the process of analyzing the places he discovers, observing them, which isn't a normal position. What I personally like about American cities—even if I wouldn't cite them as models—is that you can go through them without thinking about the architecture. You don't think about the aesthetic side, with its history, and so on. You can move within them as if you were in a desert, as if you were in a bunch of other things, without thinking about this whole business of art, aesthetics, the history of art, the history of architecture. American cities enable us to return to a kind of primal scene of space. Naturally, in spite of everything, this architecture is also structured by various realities, but in terms of their actual presence, those cities, as pure event, pure object, avoid the pretense of self-conscious architecture.

J.B. The same is true in art, in painting. In art the strongest works are those that abandon this whole business of art and art history and aesthetics. In writing, it's the same thing. Within that overaestheticized dimension, with its pretense of meaning, reality, truth, I like most when it is most invisible. I think that good architecture can do this as well; it's not so much a grieving process as a process of disappearance, of controlling disappearance as much as appearance.

Values of Functionalism

J.N. We need to recognize that we're surrounded by a great deal of accidental architecture. And an entire series of modern, or modernist, attitudes—in the historical sense—have been founded on this particular reality. There are countless numbers of sites whose aesthetic lacks any sense of intention. We find this same phenomenon outside of architecture; it's a value of functionalism. Today, when we look at a race car, we don't primarily think about its beauty. Nineteenth-century architecture is what it is, and three-quarters of the time it's not marked by any kind of aesthetic intentionality. The same applies to industrial zones at the end of the twentieth century, which are, for all intents and purposes, radical architectural forms, without concessions, abrupt, in which we can definitely locate a certain charm.

But I want to get back to your ideas about architecture, since you've definitely expressed an opinion about it. For example, you write that "in architecture the situation must be looked at backwards, we need to identify a rule." You also wrote, "In architecture the accompanying idea is a strategic minimum." And "New York is the epicenter of the end of the world. . . . As intellectuals we must work to save that end-of-the-world utopia." In any case, you're part of that effort.

New York or Utopia

J.B. When I refer to New York as the epicenter of the end of the world, I'm referring to an apocalypse. At the same time, it's a way of looking at it as a realized utopia. This is the paradox of reality. We can dream about apocalypse, but it's a perspective, something unrealizable, whose power lies in the fact that it isn't realized. New York provides the kind of stupefaction characterized by a world that is already accomplished, an absolutely apocalyptic world, but one that is replete in its verticality—and in this sense, ultimately, it engenders a form of deception because it is embodied, because it's already there, and we can no longer destroy it. It's indestructible. The form is played out, it's outlived its own usefulness, it's been realized even beyond its own limits. There's even a kind of liberation, a destructuring of space that no longer serves as a limit to verticality or, as in other places, horizontality. But does architecture still exist when space has become infinitely indeterminate in every dimension?

Here, in France, we've got something different. We have a monstrous object, something insuperable, something we are unable to repeat: Beaubourg. There's nothing better than New York. Other things will happen, and we'll make the transition to a different universe, one that's much more virtual; but within its order, we'll never do better than that city, that architecture, which is, at the same time, apocalyptic. Personally, I like this completely ambiguous figure of the city, which is simultaneously catastrophic and sublime, because it has assumed an almost hieratic force.

J.N. And when you write, "As intellectuals we must work to save that end-of-the-world utopia"?

J.B. Do we really need to save ideas? At least we should save the possibility of a form. Of the idea as form. It's true that when faced with something that's overrealized, a terminus, we're reduced to ecstasy and pure contemplation. . . . It's important that we rediscover the concept in the idea, in the mental space of the idea. We've got to get back inside or go around, to the other side. Once again, perfection serves as a screen, a different type of screen. Genius would consist in destabilizing this too-perfect image.

J.N. You also said something rather astonishing about architecture: "Architecture is a mixture of nostalgia and extreme anticipation." Do you recall? Those ideas are still vital for me, but it's been fifteen years. . . . Are they still vital for you?

Architecture: Between Nostalgia and Anticipation

J.B. We're looking for the lost object, whether we're referring to meaning or language. We use language, but it's always, at the same time, a form of nostalgia, a lost object. Language in use is basically a form of anticipation, since we're already in something else. . . . We have to be in these two orders of reality: we have to confront what we've lost and anticipate what's ahead of us; that's our brand of fatality. In this sense we can never clarify things, we can never say, "OK, that's behind us" or "OK, that's ahead of us." But it's hard to understand because the idea of modernity is for all that the idea of a continuous dimension, where it's clear that the past and the future coexist. . . . We ourselves may no longer be in that world—if we ever were!—for it may be no more than a kind of apparition. This seems to be true for any kind of form. Form is always already lost, then always already seen as something beyond itself. It's the essence of radicality. . . . It involves being radical in loss, and radical in anticipation—any object can be grasped in this way. My comments need to be contrasted with the idea that something could be "real" and that we could consider it as having a meaning, a context, a subject, an object. We know that things are no longer like that, and even the things we take to be the simplest always have an enigmatic side, which is what makes them radical.

J.N. I don't want to torture you any longer, but I'd like to read three other quotes: "Architecture consists in working against a background of spatial deconstruction." And "All things are curves." That's a very important sentence for me. And finally "Provocation would be much too serious a form of seduction." You said that in reference to architecture, by the way.

(Always) Seduction, Provocation, Secrets

J.B. Fortunately I haven't reread all those books. "All things are curves." That's the easiest to start with because there are no end points or the end points connect in a curved mirror. All things, in this sense, fulfill their own cycle.

Provocation, seduction ... Programmed seduction doesn't exist, so it doesn't mean much. Seduction should, nevertheless, contain some sense of that antagonism, that countercurrent; it should both have the sense and implement it.... Here too any concerted effort at implementation is obviously contradictory. Seduction can't be programmed, and disappearance, whether of constructed things or generalized ambivalence, can't be officialized. It has to remain secret. The order of secrecy, which is the order of seduction, obviously exists only through provocation; it's almost exactly the opposite. Provocation is an attempt to make something visible through contradiction, through scandal, defiance; to make something visible that should perhaps guard its secret. The problem is to achieve this law or this rule. The rule is really the secret, and the secret obviously becomes increasingly difficult in a world like our own, where everything is given to us totally promiscuously, so that there are no gaps, no voids, no nothingness; nothingness no longer exists, and nothingness is where secrecy happens, the place where things lose their meaning, their identity—not only would they assume all possible meanings here, but they would remain truly unintelligible in some sense.

I think that in every building, every street, there is something that creates an event, and whatever creates an event is unintelligible. This can also occur in situations or in individual behavior; it's something you don't realize, something you can't program. You have more experience than I do with urban projects, which arrange spatial freedom, the space of freedom; all those programs are obviously absolutely contradictory. So, at bottom, the secret exists wherever people hide it. It's also possible in dualistic, ambivalent relations, for at that moment something becomes unintelligible once again, like some precious material.

J.N. We can continue by talking about the aesthetics of disappearance. I'd like to quote you once again, but this time not with respect to architecture, and I want to provoke you a little as well. You write, "If being a nihilist is being obsessed by the mode of disappearance rather than the mode of production, then I'm a nihilist." You also write, "I am for everything that is opposed to culture." This brings us back in a way to certain contemporary issues. . . . I can say the same thing about architecture: I'm for everything that is opposed to architecture. Twenty years ago I began a book that way: "The future of architecture is not architectural." The key is to agree on what architecture is . . . and where it's going. The key is to agree on what culture is and where it's going.

The Metamorphosis of Architecture

J.N. Architecture is pretty easy. Let me explain. One of the things I consider essential is the idea that there has been a complete change in architecture during this century, in the sense that architecture had as its initial goal the construction of the artificial world in which we live. This happened rather simply—there was an independent body of knowledge, something clear, there were recipes. Vitruvius produced a book of recipes; he tells you exactly how to construct a building, the number of columns, the proportions, and so on. Academicism consisted in improving the use of these ingredients slightly. There were instructions for building cities as well; architects made use of different typologies, different recipes for urban art, et cetera. Then, suddenly, there was a shift in the demographics. You're quite familiar with this. Everyone moved to the cities, the cities exploded, we tried to maintain a certain number of rules, which were generally based on planning. These too exploded one after the other. We have experienced a kind of urban big bang and find that we are unable to use the existing recipes. Everything associated with those existing recipes, in other words, architecture with a capital "A," has become absolutely ridiculous. As soon as you integrate a structural model into this system, it becomes absurd.

So in this sense, I'm against everything that is part of the same order as Architecture. This means that from this point on, we must make use of another strategy, where we're required to be slightly more intelligent—to the extent that we can be—required to constantly diagnose the situation, required to face the fact that architecture is no longer the invention of a world but that it exists simply with respect to a geological layer applied to all the cities throughout the planet.... Architecture can no longer have as its goal the transformation, the modification, of this accumulated material. For some, it's intolerable; they feel like they've been fired. From the moment we initiate this discourse, however, it's as if we were against a form of ancestral culture; we throw out the baby with the bathwater. You can't generate any positive effect within this framework. Some go even further. We're faced with the generic city; that's the way it is, and there's nothing to be done about it.

I suspect that you're pretty much in agreement with this type of approach, which, by the way, I happen to understand. Yet I've still maintained a certain residue of optimism.... I think that through small movements we can achieve an ethics whereby the situation becomes slightly more positive every time we intervene. We can try to locate a kind of enjoyment of place by including things that weren't considered previously, which are frequently accidental, and inventing strategies of improvement, the poetics of situations; we can evaluate completely random elements and declare that we're dealing with a geography: "It's beautiful. I'm going to reveal it to you...." This is an aesthetics of revelation, a way of taking a piece of the world and saying, "I'm appropriating this, and I'm giving it back to you for your appreciation in a different way." In this century, architecture finds itself faced with incommensurable, metaphysical dimensions. A priori it can't do anything about that. It's in the same situation as philosophy or science: it's now an adult. We need to develop other strategies.

At this point, we need to take into account the fatal dimensions of place, the deflection of what we're about to do, evaluate a number of possibles in terms of scenarios, and tell ourselves that what we're about to do is going to be part of a becoming that is hidden to us. . . . This is the opposite of the architecture that's still being taught in nine out of ten schools. It may look like an attitude against architecture, but that's not the case . . . just as when you wrote, rather unconditionally, "I'm for everything that is opposed to culture."

The Aesthetics of Modernity

J.B. I was referring to culture in the sense of aestheticization, and I am opposed to such aestheticization because it inevitably involves a loss: the loss of the object, of this secret that works of art and creative effort might reveal and which is something more than aesthetics. The secret can't be aesthetically unveiled. It's the kind of "punctum" Barthes spoke of in reference to photography—its secret, something inexplicable and nontransmissible, something that is in no way interactive. It's something that's there and not there at the same time. Within culture this thing is completely dissipated, volatilized. Culture involves the total legibility of everything in it, and what's more, it comes into being at the very moment Duchamp transposed a very simple object, the urinal, into an art object. He transposed its banality to create an event within the aesthetic universe and deaestheticize it. He forced banality upon it—he broke into the home of aesthetics—and stopped it cold. Paradoxically he made possible the generalized aestheticization that typifies the modern era. And I wonder whether this form of acting out on Duchamp's part, in the field of painting, which wasn't a revolution but an implosion, had an equivalent in the architectural universe. Is there a kind of before and after among forms? Here too, it's still the end of a kind of modernity, which began at the moment everything that was considered energy, or the forces of modernity—whether these involved society, social wealth, industry—was oriented by the idea of progress. The idea of art history in some form, of the progress of art, hung on in art.

With abstraction we had the impression that a liberation had taken place, an orgy of modernity. That all broke apart in a kind of sudden implosion, a leveling of the aesthetic's sense of the sublime. And in the end, when this aesthetic of the secret disappeared, we had culture.

Culture

J.B. Culture is everywhere. In any case, at this point in time, it's a homologue of industry and technology. It's a mental technique, a mental technology that was embellished through architectural services, museums, et cetera. In the case of photography, I was interested in this history at one point. . . . When Barthes spoke about photography, he brought up the question of the "punctum." Through this punctum, the photograph becomes an event in our head, in our mental life, where it is something different, a singular relation, an absolute singularity. This punctum, which, according to Barthes, is a nonplace, nothing, the nothingness at the heart of the photograph, disappeared, and in its place we constructed a museum of photography. This death, which Barthes said was the heart of the photograph, the photograph itself, the symbolic power of the photograph, disappeared, it assumed the shape of a monument or a museum, and this time a concrete death materialized. This was a cultural operation, and that operation, yes, I am against it, emphatically, with no concessions, without compromise.

We are stuck in an unlimited, metastatic development of culture, which has heavily invested in architecture. But to what extent can we judge it? Today it's very difficult to identify, in a given building, what belongs to this secret, this singularity that hasn't really disappeared. I think that as a form it is indestructible but is increasingly consumed by culture. Is any voluntary, conscious resistance possible? Yes. I think that each of us can resist. But it would be difficult for such resistance to become political. I don't get the impression there could be any organized political resistance as such. It would always be an exception, and whatever you do will always be "exceptional" in that sense.

A work of art is a singularity, and all these singularities can create holes, interstices, voids, et cetera, in the metastatic fullness of culture. But I don't see them coalescing, combining into a kind of antipower that could invest the other. No. We are definitively immersed in the order of culture, that is, until the apocalypse arrives. We can, I think, combine all this within the same concept. I think that even political economy in the form it has assumed, which is also completely skewed, and which is not at all a principle of economic reality but one of pure speculation, a political economy that culminates in a speculative void, is an aesthetic. Now, Walter Benjamin already analyzed this in the field of politics. In that sense, we are witnessing an aestheticization of behavior and structure. But aestheticization is not part of the real; on the contrary, it signifies that things are becoming values, assume value. We can no longer compare an interplay of forms. It's unintelligible and can't be assigned any ultimate meaning, because it's a game, a rule, something different. With generalized aestheticization, forms are exhausted and become value. But value, aesthetics, culture, et cetera, are infinitely negotiable, and everyone can benefit, although here we are within the domain of order and equivalence, the complete leveling of all singularity. I believe we are part of that order, from which nothing can escape. But I also still feel that singularities as such can function even though they assume what are frequently monstrous forms—for example, those "monsters" you spoke about. What interests me is architecture as monster, those objects that have been catapulted into the city, from someplace else. In a way I appreciate this monstrous character. The first was Beaubourg. We could provide a cultural description of Beaubourg, consider Beaubourg as the synthesis of this total "culturization," and, in this case, be completely opposed to it. Nonetheless the Beaubourg object is a singular event in our history, a monster. And it is a monster because it demonstrates nothing, it's a monster, and in that sense a kind of singularity.

It's obvious that such objects, whether architectural or not, escape their programmed existence, the future you have given them. . . . This metamorphosis can become a singular personal intuition or the result of an overall effect that no one intended.

Still, the object (architectural or not) in question will produce a gaping hole in this culturality.

A Heroic Architectural Act?

J.N. We might ask ourselves why there is no equivalent to Duchamp in the world of architecture. There is no equivalent because there is no auto-architecture. There is no architect who could make an immediate, scandalous gesture that was accepted. Architects have tried to confront these limits—that was the starting point of postmodernity. We could say that in his own way, Venturi tried to do it. He took the simplest building that existed, a basic building from the suburbs of Philadelphia—even the location wasn't important, it was the least significant location possible—made of brick, with standard windows, and so on, and he said: "This is the architecture we must make today." And his gesture implied an entire theory, a theory that was opposed to the heroic architectural act, although in terms of derision it was a "weak" application of the dadaist revolution (on the Richter scale, it was one or two; Duchamp is seven). But all these attempts culminated in notable failures, since we as architects are unable to attain the same distance from the object. I have no idea what would enable us to identify Duchamp's fountain if it weren't in a museographic space. It demands certain reading conditions and a certain distance, which don't exist for architecture. At most we could say that this act of complete vulgarization might occur in spite of the client's intentions. The only problem is that if you do that and you repeat it, it becomes insignificant. No further reality, no further reading of the act is possible; you've become part of the total disappearance of the architectural act.

J.B. Duchamp's act also becomes insignificant, wants to be insignificant, wants insignificance, and becomes insignificant in spite of itself through repetition, as well as through all of Duchamp's by-products. The event itself is unique, singular, and that's the end of it. It's ephemeral. Afterward there's a whole string of them, in art as well, since from that moment on, the path was cleared for the resurgence of earlier forms; postmodernism, if you like. The moment simply existed.

Art, Architecture, and Postmodernity

J.N. So can this debate about contemporary art—"it's junk, worthless"—be applied to architecture? Can it be extrapolated?

J.B. I'd like to ask you the same thing.

J.N. I'd say that the search for limits and the pleasure of destruction are part of both art and architecture. You were talking about the idea of destruction as something that can be positive. This search for a limit, this search for nothingness, almost nothingness, takes place within the search for something positive; that is, we're looking for the essence of something. This search for an essence reaches limits that are near the limits of perception and the evacuation of the visible. We no longer experience pleasure through the eye but through the mind. A white square on a white background is a type of limit. James Turrel is a type of limit. Does that mean it's worthless? In the case of James Turrel, you enter a space, and it's monochromatic. Is it one step further than Klein? Is that why you're fascinated? You know there's nothing there, you feel there's nothing there, you can even pass your hand through it, and you're fascinated by the object in a way because it's the essence of something. Once he's given us the keys to his game, he does the same thing with a square of blue sky. He's currently working on the crater of a volcano, where, when you lie down at the bottom of the crater, you can see the perfect circle of the cosmos. All of these ideas are based on a certain search for the limit of nothingness. So when you leave the Venice Biennale, realizing that this search for nothingness has ended in worthlessness, that's a critical judgment I can share in 80 percent of the cases. However, the history of art has always consisted of a majority of minor works.

J.B. This search for nothingness is, on the contrary, the aestheticized fact of wanting this nothingness to have an existence, a value, and even, at some point, a surplus value, without considering the market, which soon takes control of it. It's the opposite in one sense. . . . Duchamp's gesture was to reduce things to insignificance. In a way, he's not responsible for what happened afterward. So when other artists take possession of this "nothingness" or, through this nothingness, take possession of banality, waste, the world, the real world, and they transfigure the banal reality of the world into an aesthetic object, it's their choice, and it's worthless in that sense, but it's also annoying, because I would rather associate an aura with worthlessness, with "nothingness." This nothingness is in fact something. It's what hasn't been aestheticized. It's what, one way or another, can't be reduced to any form of aestheticization. Rather, it's this highly focused strategy of nothingness and worthlessness that I am opposed to. The difference between Warhol and the others, who did the same thing—although it isn't the same thing—is based on the fact that he takes an image and reduces it to nothing. He uses the technical medium to reveal the insignificance, the lack of objectivity, the illusion of the image itself. And then other artists make use of the technique to re-create an aesthetic in other technological media, through science itself, through scientific images. They reproduce the aesthetic. They do exactly the opposite of what Warhol was able to do, they reaestheticize the technique, while Warhol, through technique, revealed technique itself as a radical illusion.

Here the term "worthlessness" is ambivalent, ambiguous. It can refer to the best or the worst. Personally, I assign great importance to worthlessness in the sense of nothingness, in the sense that, if we achieve this art of disappearance, we've achieved art, whereas all the strategy used to manage most of the stuff we're shown—where there's usually nothing to see in any event—serves precisely to convert that worthlessness into spectacle, into aesthetic, into market value, into a form of complete unconsciousness, the collective syndrome of aestheticization known as culture. We can't say it's all the same, but the exceptions can only be moments. For me, Duchamp is one of them; Warhol is another. But there are other singularities, Francis

Bacon, perhaps, maybe others. But it's not a question of names of artists. . . . It can never be anything but a onetime event that affects us in this world saturated with values and aesthetics. From that moment on, there is no more history of art. We see that art—and this is one aspect of its worthlessness—with its retrograde history, exhausts itself in its own history trying to resuscitate all those forms, the way politics does in other areas. It's a form of regression, an interminable phase of repetition during which we can always bring back any older work of art, or style, or technique as a fashion or aesthetic—a process of endless recycling.

J.N. Couldn't we say that the twentieth century has seen a surfeit of art? Because during the century, any artist who managed to define a formal field has become a great artist? All it takes is a bit of ash on a leaf. All it takes is the ability to experience something with respect to the ash, to contextualize it, distance it, and the concept appears. . . . The artist who has succeeded in finding his field has become identifiable, gets noticed, has a market value, et cetera. This has been a century of gigantic exploration: exploration of the real, exploration of sensations, of everything around us, a search for sensation. Some succeeded; others didn't. All of this was then mixed up with meaning and with conceptual art. When Laurence Wiener hangs a sentence in space without touching it, whatever happens, happens as part of the relation between the sentence and the space. It's not a big deal, but it's a field in and of itself. We've lived through this gigantic exploration. Everyone can find their value system, has experienced events, facts, modes, and interactions that sometimes resulted in arte povera, or pop art, or conceptual art, et cetera. But all that exploration kept getting extended further, and everyone is looking for whatever they can grab. Does this mean that all this exploration is part of that "worthlessness"?

J.B. Well, there may be a history of art that's not progressive but which deepens the analytic side of art, and all abstraction is still a reduction of the visible world, of the object, into its microelements. It's a way of returning to a primal geometry. It's exactly the same thing as the search for analytic truth in the social sciences. It's the same kind of process. We've gone from the evidence of appearances to the fundamental fractal nature of things. This is the history of abstraction, and this search leads directly into another dimension, which is no longer that of appearance or a strategy of appearances, but of a need centered on in-depth analytic knowledge of the object and the world, which, in a sense, puts an end to sense relations. It's the extermination of the sensible, but it still constitutes a search, I agree.

Once we've arrived at this point, however, it's over. . . . We have an artificial reconstruction of evidence, of perception, but the crucial act, the determining factor, is abstraction. Afterward we're no longer really in a world of forms; we're in a micro-world. Art even anticipated scientific discovery; it went deeper and deeper into the fractal world, into geometry. I don't mean that all sensibility, all perception, disappeared. It's always possible for anyone, any object, to have a singular relation but not an aesthetic one, to have a primitive relation, something to do with this punctum, anyone can experience that. . . . So-called aesthetic mediation is over with. The artist is someone who exploits the domain of singularity so that he can appropriate it and use it interactively both through the market structure and through a number of other things as well. But the dualistic relation of any individual with any object, even the most worth-less, is singular, it retains its power, and it can be rediscovered. I don't feel that this has been lost; that's not the problem with the sensible, the fatal. By this I mean that the fatal relation with things, with appearances, can be rediscovered, but if it is, today that discovery will be in conflict with aesthetics, with art. In the same sense, you can rediscover a dualistic relation in society, in other domains, in alterity. But this doesn't take place through politics, or economics; those things are behind us, they have their history, and we are in another world where those mediating structures have either monopolized the entire market, and at that point should be destroyed, or have already destroyed themselves. By the way, that's what I meant when I said that "art is worthless."

Visual Disappointment, Intellectual Disappointment

J.N. Aren't you as disappointed visually as you are intellectually? In your writing, you tell your readers that you would prefer to be deaf than blind, and just how important sight is for you. But paradoxically one has the impression that a certain amount of vacuity or disappearance might interest you. Isn't it with respect to the voyeur, or observer, in you that you believe the art object is vacuous? Doesn't [Robert] Ryman, doesn't [Ad] Reinhardt, disappoint your senses before disappointing you intellectually?

J.B. I agree with you completely. Seen from another viewpoint, it's true that I don't believe there is any relation whatsoever between an image and a text, between writing and the visual. If there is an affinity, it would occur through a more secretive network than anything we perceive, by fortuitous correspondences, as has always been the case. Image and text are two singular registers; we need to maintain their singularity. The same thing can be represented in either way; the interplay of forms can be represented in either of them, but they can't ever be correlated. For me, something of the fantastic remains in the image. Any image retains something of the savage and fantastic. What I would like is that it retain that character. But today images have been aestheticized, they have become increasingly virtualized, they are no longer images. Television is the opposite of the image: there are no images on television. Yes, I'm visually disappointed, and painting has exactly the same effect on me. To me they're digitally synthesized images, technically and mentally, but they're no longer images. Once again the possibility exists to re-create the primal scene, the original savagery of the image, but starting from nothing, any intuition, in the literal sense of the term, can re-create the image. For example, this punctum, this secret associated with the image, I sometimes find it in photography. So we're not desperate. But the disappointment in the contextual universe that surrounds us, with images bombarding us from every side, yes, I resent that.

J.N. I have the impression that the sense of something's being "worthless, worthless, worthless" in architecture also exists! It is just as overwhelming but, paradoxically, perhaps for the opposite reason. That is to say, what characterizes this worthless architecture today, three-quarters of the time, is the "picturesque." Or it's the extension of a private model of meaning and sensibility. One of the current dramas in architecture is modeling, cloning. Often we don't know what to do; the context is hopeless. Not only the geographic, urban context, but the human context as well, the context of the commission, the financial context, everything is hopeless. And trained architects are forced to confront that reality. That reminds me of something Judd was saying, "I looked in the El Paso phone book. There are twenty-five hundred architects, and I've never seen any architecture in El Paso!" A great number of architects borrow a model that comes from a magazine, or a contractor or client. And at that moment, we have to identify a number of existing parameters that are reassuring, because if we do architecture, we want it to be seen, and at the same time we don't want to make waves. However, the majority of architectures produced today aren't based on those simple, clean, savage, radical rules that you talk about in your book on New York. Most of the time, they're a collage of objects, the one that presents the fewest problems either for the one who's designing it, or for the one who's receiving it, or for the builder. And for those three reasons, it's worthless, worthless, worthless. We're looking for something else.

Maybe we're looking for that aesthetic of disappearance that Paul Virilio discusses. But not necessarily in the sense Virilio intends, in that virtual, informatic space where information circulates rather than humans, not in a virtual space because those objects are completely lacking in meaning. That's the primary characteristic of everything being built today, and the paradox is that the most poetic things are, on the social level, the most dramatic. That is, the most authentic things, the truest, will be found in the cities of the South, where they are made out of necessity, but also in connection with a culture that's very much alive. These aren't objects that are parachuted in, inauthentic objects that correspond to some architectural convention. The problem of the worthlessness of architecture presents itself with at least the same acuity as in the field of art, but certainly not on the same basis.

The Aesthetics of Disappearance

J.B. Obviously we need to be clear about what we mean by the aesthetics of disappearance. . . . It's true that there are a thousand ways to disappear, but we can at least compare the kind of disappearance that results in extermination—which is one of the ideas underlying Paul Virilio's work—and the way things disappear in a "network," which affects all of us and could be considered a kind of sublimation. The disappearance I'm talking about, which results in the concept of worthlessness or nothingness I mentioned earlier, means that one form disappears into another. It's a kind of metamorphosis: appearance– disappearance. The mechanism is completely different. It's not the same as disappearing within a network, where everyone becomes the clone or metastasis of something else; it's a chain of interlinked forms, into which we disappear, where everything implies its own disappearance. It's all about the art of disappearance. Unfortunately there's only one word to describe it, and the same is true for the term "worthlessness." We can use it in different senses, just as we can the term "nothingness," but no matter what happens, we enter a field of discourse that can no longer be fully explained, we've got to play the game, we're forced to.

Images of Modernity

J.N. Do you still have a positive outlook on modernity?

J.B. Did I ever?

J.N. You did, and you're going to jump when I tell you because it's something you wrote, and it's not nihilist at all. In fact, it's rather optimistic, since you talk about modernity as the "activism of well-being."

J.B. I get the impression you're still talking about a prior life. That's pretty good! . . . Well-being, it was an old concept even then; now I think we're beyond happiness. The problem is no longer the identification of coherence among needs, objects, all those things . . . upon which a certain conception of architecture also depended, by the way. That's been "nullified," but in the sense of having disappeared inside a network. We no longer ask if we're happy or not. Within a network, you're simply part of the chain, and you move from one terminal to another; you're "transported," in a way, but you're not necessarily happy.

The question of happiness, like that of freedom or responsibility, and a host of other questions about modernity, the ideals of modernity—these are no longer really relevant, at least in terms of expecting a response. In that sense, I'm no longer modern. If modernity is conceived in this way, which was to subjectively ensure—whether it was the subjectivity of the individual or the group—a maximum of accumulation, a maximal number of things, then modernity has overshot the goal it set for itself. Maybe it didn't fail at all, maybe it succeeded all too well, it propelled us well beyond our goal . . . and now all the questions are about lost objects.

The Biology of the Visible

J.N. Concepts of modernity in architecture are very ambiguous because they are tied to historical concepts, whereas modernity by its very nature is something vital, although today I think it is primarily concerned with the aesthetic forms of disappearance. I read "Every real thing is prepared to disappear, that's all it asks for." I feel that in the field of architecture, and, more than architecture, design in the broadest sense, we are experiencing an aesthetic of "sacrifice." I would say, the sacrifice of the visual. I don't know where it's leading, but part of it is reflected in miniaturization, our increasing domination of matter, with matter itself being increasingly reduced to its simplest expression. It's quite obvious that for objects like the computer, which has been miniaturized to an astounding degree, compared to the cathode-ray screen, the television, it's eventually going to end up as thin as a piece of rolling paper. We can't see these things as they happen; we can only see the result. That's all we have. When we're successful, all we have is action, the means to achieve it are obliterated, they cease to be interesting. This century once looked into the mirror of a mechanistic modernity and grew excited at looking inside things—motors, gears, cutaway drawings—now that's over with, it no longer interests us, all we want is the result. That's a disturbing kind of miracle.

J.B. You're forgetting that we're still looking inside the genetic code, trying to decode genes, et cetera. We want to make those kinds of things visible, but there's no mechanism. Whether the research takes place in the field of biology or genetics, the fantasy is the same. . . . I don't know if it's the culmination of modernity or an excrescence. Maybe this effort to get at the analytic heart of things, this desire to reveal the interior of matter itself, until we reach those particles that, at times, are completely invisible, will eventually lead us to immateriality or, in any case, to something that can no longer be represented: particles, molecules, et cetera. Practically speaking, in biology, for us, it's pretty much the same thing, except that we've transposed to the human all our efforts at microanalysis, fractalization, et cetera. . . . In a way, it's modernity that has reduced itself to its most basic elements, ultimately culminating in an algebra of the invisible.

J.N. . . . whose complexity is one of the essential paradigms.

J.B. These are elements that are "elsewhere" in the sense that they are no longer perceptible, no longer part of perception or representation. But they are not "elsewhere" in the sense that they come from another place, in the sense that they might really represent another form, which we would have to deal with in dualistic terms. If beings from another place were to appear, there would be a renewed possibility of interaction, but even here, no interaction is possible on the level of the code, of genetics, basic elements, et cetera. There is no more interaction. True, there is infinite combination, and we'll go as far as we can in that direction—not despairingly, of course. No, quite the contrary. There's even a kind of collective fascination with the image that this reality offers us in return. But we can no longer claim that some notion of happiness or freedom will ultimately be involved, because they've disappeared, they've volatilized into that analytic research we've been talking about. So is that the end of modernity?

A New Hedonism?

J.N. We can have a more optimistic vision of things . . . especially once we manage to dominate matter in such a way that it enables us to resolve practical problems, problems tied to certain kinds of pleasure, even if the initial pleasure is perverted by excess. . . . The wireless telephone is a good example. You can call anywhere in the world from any other point in the world, just as it's possible today to press on a piece of glass and make it transparent or opaque and feel your hand warm up on contact. Everything takes place over a surface of a few millimeters. . . . Such technological innovations are heading in the direction of new sensations and added comfort, in the direction of new forms of pleasure. So maybe the situation isn't as desperate as all that!

J.B. I wasn't talking about despair. I simply find that there is a strange attraction, a fascination with such things. . . . Is fascination a form of happiness? For me it is, but it's not the happiness associated with seduction; it's something else. The vertigo that pushes us to go further and further in that direction exists, clearly, and we all share in it collectively, but we have to make sure that when we reach the boundaries of our explorations, we don't trigger processes that are completely obliterating. When we reach the micro-micro, even in biology, we end up triggering viruses. They may have been there all along, but we've managed to reactivate them, we've brought them back to life. We discovered them, but they discovered us as well, and there are all sorts of ways things can backfire, including those that lead to what may be a kind of fatal reversibility. We are no longer the masters. I don't like to play prophet, but we shouldn't believe that all these analytic advances will lead to greater control of the world, or to increased happiness. On the contrary, even science recognizes that it has less and less control over the real, the object ceases to exist—at some point it simply disappears. So where do we look? OK, so it's a bit like that ideal object discussed during the Enlightenment: progress, the rights of man, and all the rest. . . . So there we have our object. That doesn't mean it's been lost. It's still a nostalgic vision, it's just that it's come apart, it's been dispersed, when what we wanted was to force it into its ultimate reality. And in that sense it has disappeared, it's gone, although it may come back under a different form, a fatal form, in the worst sense of the word—we just don't know. . . . What's going to happen with all the negative exponential processes that have been triggered and which we know are moving much more quickly than the positive processes? In any case, the outlook, if there is one, is one of complete ambiguity. That's truly the end of modernity. As long as modernity was able to believe that there was still a positive direction and the negative would be buried deeper and deeper in positivity, we were still very much in line with modernity. But once everything we're searching for becomes ambiguous, ambivalent, reversible, random, then modernity is over—and it's just as true for politics.

II
Second Interview

Truth in Architecture

Jean Baudrillard: Can we speak of truth in architecture? No, at least not in the sense that architecture would have truth as its goal or culmination. There are things an architecture wants to say, things it claims to accomplish, signify. . . . Where is the radicality of architecture? What is it that constitutes the radicality of architecture? That's how we should pose the question of truth in architecture. That truth is to some extent what architecture is trying to achieve without wanting to say it—which is a form of involuntary radicality. In other words, it's what the user makes of it, what happens to it through use, when in the grip of an uncontrollable actor. This leads me to introduce another aspect of things, which is their literality. To my mind, literality means that aside from technical progress, aside from social and historical development, the architectural object as an event that has taken place is no longer susceptible to being completely interpreted or explained. Such objects express things literally, in the sense that no exhaustive interpretation is possible.

*is this
necessarily
true?*

*what would
constitute
otherwise*

What does "literally" mean? I'll use the example of Beaubourg again. OK, we have Beaubourg. So what does it express? Culture, communication? No, I don't think so. Beaubourg expresses flux, storage, redistribution, and Piano and Rogers's architecture expresses those things literally. What it expresses literally is almost the reverse of the message it supposedly expresses. Beaubourg represents both the fact of culture and the thing that killed culture, the thing it succumbed to, in other words, the confusion of signs, the excess, the profusion. It's this internal contradiction that translates Beaubourg's architecture, which I call its "literality." Similarly, we can say that the World Trade Center alone expresses the spirit of New York City in its most radical form: verticality. The towers are like two perforated strips. They are the city itself and, at the same time, the vehicle by means of which the city as a historical and symbolic form has been liquidated—repetition, cloning. The twin towers are clones of each other. It's the end of the city, but it's a very beautiful end, and architecture expresses both, both the end and the fulfillment of that end. That finality, which is both symbolic and real, and situated well outside the project that the architect's drawing embodied, far beyond the initial definition of the architectural object, is expressed *literally.*

Another Tower for Beaubourg

Jean Nouvel: It's worth asking if Beaubourg really signified culture. . . . When you look at Beaubourg from within the world of architecture, you realize that it's one of the first attempts to concretize the theory of Archigram's city-as-machine. In a way, Beaubourg is the culmination of functionalist theories, where architecture translates the truth of the building, which is a kind of hypertruth. The skeleton is visible, with all its guts on the outside, and the nerves, everything is exposed to view, to a degree that's never been surpassed. English high-tech reached a peak in the seventies, but Beaubourg is the only building that took so much of a risk, aside from the Lloyds building, perhaps, which shares the same sense of exhibitionism. Richard Rogers extended the movement to factories. . . . But the most interesting thing in the Beaubourg concept, originally, was the freedom within, in the way the space was conceived. We felt that this machine for housing art—or hopefully for manufacturing art—was going to work. Completely unpredictable events were supposed to take place within the building, the floor areas were supposed to coexist with added sections, supports, movable extensions, everything was supposed to be optimally organized within a dialectic of support-supply. Beaubourg was primarily a support. But the space, subsequently made "functional," completely altered its initial meaning. It's worth pointing out that in January 1999 an ad was designed—while they were working on the restoration—which for the first time completely covered the facade with an enormous photograph on canvas that was more than two hundred meters long and thirty meters high. Beaubourg's mission is to capture these exterior and interior events, events of all kinds, which are supposed to be free or of limited duration. The implosion you spoke about occurred in a completely unexpected way. The thing that was killed before it even got off the ground was the exposure to other possibilities, the play inherent in the possibilities of space, its total vacuity. The fact that they reconstructed the interior space using ordinary partitions, turning it into a space that is completely conventional, meant that Beaubourg would become the opposite of a simple architectural support, to the extent that they've now put G-strings on the beams so they appear more dignified, so they can erase any industrial or mechanical reference! Every freedom that existed within the space has been wrecked by the fire department, which insisted that the floor area, which was 150 by 50 meters—which is huge!—be divided by a wall. The space was simply cut in two. This alteration alone removed the necessity, and therefore the meaning, of putting the ducts on the outside—they could just as well have been stuck inside the service core or between two walls. But in the beginning it was much more relevant. Everything that was supposed to interact with this support and change rapidly didn't happen, and Beaubourg is experienced as if it were a building made of dressed stone. Because it was overconsumed, because of the incredible number of visitors every year, its enormous size, the building has been exhausted very quickly. This accelerated aging is also a characteristic of the building. But it's interesting to see the enormous discrepancy between the architectural intentions and the reality. At the same time, it was Renzo Piano, one of the two architects who designed Beaubourg, who is responsible for the building's restoration—if you can call it that—in its current, rather than its conceptual, state. It's difficult to imagine the energy of the seventies today.

J.B. Yet in its flexibility, Beaubourg did reflect its original intent.

J.N. No, it hasn't played its role; the building is static. Maybe it will happen one day. . . . But no one wanted to play with that flexibility; it was too dangerous, too spontaneous. Everything has been reframed, resealed. Imagine a building with large windows built in 1930. The same thing would have happened then, assuming there was a large flat roof with a beautiful belvedere. Of course, its status as an urban artifact remains. Beaubourg functions as a cathedral, with its buttresses, a nave, a "piazza." It's a call to the public to come inside, to consume the views of Paris and the art. A call to consumption.

[margin handwritten note: Consumption vs. over-consumption of Architecture]

[handwritten annotation: circled text "to consume the views of Paris and the art. A call to consumption."]

A Shelter for Culture?

J.B. Yes, it's also a draft of air pulling things along in its wake. And locally it's still a kind of hole, an air inlet. . . . As for sheltering or provoking culture, I'm skeptical. . . . How can you recapture the subversiveness that the space seemed to call forth as it was originally designed?

J.N. Can the institution accept subversion? Can it plan the unknown, the unforeseeable? Can it, within a space as open as this, provide artists with the conditions for something that is oversized, an interference; can it agree to not set limits? Architecture is one thing; human life another. What good is an architecture that is out of step with contemporary life?

[handwritten note: what are limits to acceptably violate]

J.B. Still, even though we can effectively express the relationship of architecture, or a given building, to culture, to society . . . how are we going to define its "social" impact? It's precisely the lack of a possible definition of the social that should produce an architecture of the indefinable, in other words, a real-time architecture, characterized by randomness and the uncertainty that drives social life. Architecture can no longer "monumental-ize" anything today. . . . But it can't demonumentalize anything either, so what role does it play?

J.N. Some people have tried to provoke this real-time, random architecture. We're trying to do this in an industrial building that everyone finds hideous, although it's absolutely remark-able: a group of derelict buildings that no one wanted, a Seita factory. It's an abandoned factory complex, located in one of the most popular quarters of Marseilles, known as "la Belle de mai." Eighty thousand square meters of empty space! The place was empty and unsafe. The city was handling security, and people had begun to squat in the buildings, until one day, quite spon-taneously, the artists got involved—people from theater, cho-reographers, painters and sculptors. So now there was a clear desire to create a kind of open cultural space, based on a living culture, just the opposite of the kinds of buildings that are usu-ally reserved for culture, with scheduled hours, and designed for conservation. The place would be open day and night, the artists would live there, some would be invited as a group by producers and would have an opportunity to continue their work jointly. There was a clear mandate for the project to initiate new work, giving preference to younger artists, creators, students, the un-employed, with a very clear intercultural dimension. But this type of approach and this type of architecture have the greatest difficulty obtaining financing, and funding for maintenance and development. The contradiction is difficult to resolve be-cause the people who start the project would prefer not to get involved in some sort of institutional operation, but they're required to ask for approval, for permission from institutions, whether they involve the city or the government—which reject such radicality. Nonetheless I think the project is part of the dynamic of what must become a contemporary cultural space. The hypercentralized, hyperinstitutionalized places we're surrounded with are sterile.

On Modification: Mutation or Rehabilitation

J.N. I think the debate going on about what I call "modification" is essential. We built heavily throughout the century, very quickly, very badly, anywhere, anyhow. We produced and reproduced a number of things in record time: spaces, buildings, suburbs, and nonplaces as well. Now we're in a situation, in all the northern countries, where growth is just about over. But urban and suburban spaces, the rural landscape, et cetera, are subject to constant modification. We find ourselves with a body of architectural material—things that were built, abandoned, rebuilt—which have to be modified or demolished; in any case, that's what we have to work with. It's not a question of any prior intention to conserve a certain number of signs of the past, nor of "rehabilitating," in the conventional sense of the term, some sort of "refined bourgeois taste, the essence of the picturesque." It's about creating architecture, meaning and essence, from some raw, unworked material. If we look at what's going on in Marseilles, we see an industrial building that could be considered a cultural facility that is 80 percent complete. The simple fact of changing its use and sticking a certain number of objects inside, applying a few finishing touches, various architectural signs, alters the meaning of the place completely. To give you an example, there were large rooms 150 meters long and 40 meters wide. Before, the space was saturated with machine tools; now that it's empty, it's sumptuous. It would be impossible to create a cultural space like that from scratch today. It would cost too much. We chose to consider this interior-exterior urban ensemble as a piece of the city. People live there as if it were a small city. And we feel that the architectural act revolves around settling into a repurposed architecture. This could involve something that's built inside or on the roof or even on a terrace. Nonetheless this process of sedimentation is a form of creation and a complete qualification of the space. It's not only a modification; it's a mutation. The space is no longer experienced the same way, there are different things inside; we play with scale differently, change the meaning, and starting with what was a large, poorly defined, purely functional volume, we've gradually managed to produce a regenerative re-creation that no one would have thought possible. This process of fabricating cities today should be encouraged. It allows us to escape dimensional standards, to obtain this sense of "excess," this superfluity that is essential and unplanned. It provokes a sense of excess: too big, too high, too dark, too ugly, too stiff, unforeseen, radical.

J.B. But this mutation, as you call it, is often part of a cultural plan. In fact, what we call "cultural" is ultimately only a bunch of polymorphous or, who knows, perverse activities!

J.N. When the mutation isn't really a mutation, it becomes perverse; it becomes rehabilitation. Rehabilitation, in the legal sense of the term, is the process of providing something with qualities that had been denied to it previously. In fact, all the public housing built during the sixties and seventies has now been "rehabilitated," which means that they're maintained—something that had been overlooked for years—that someone applies a little color to the facade, a couple of awnings, and that "ghettoization" is perpetuated by allowing the urban social fabric around them to degrade and violence to spread. We continue to promote an approach to housing that we know doesn't work, and we solidify and perpetuate all the problems we have. Moreover, to reduce costs, we contract the work out to companies who cap expenses as much as possible. The building is insulated on the outside. We pretend to make a number of improvements, when all we've done is patched things up: we touch it up here and there, and it's good for another twenty years, even though the buildings were only designed to last twenty years when they were built.

J.B. The large urban spaces that have sprung into existence without any preliminary planning, like New York's Lower East Side or Soho, have been taken over by the middle class over the past twenty years, often artists, who have changed the lifestyle and appearance of those neighborhoods: is that rehabilitation or mutation? It's easy to see that this kind of mutation is most often accompanied by a gentrification of the neighborhood, which was also the case in Salvador da Bahia, in Brazil. They saved the facades, but behind those facades, everything changed.

J.N. Look at Paris, for example. This city has been characterized by what I call "embalming." This consists in preserving a series of facades that have some historic value and building new structures behind them—this happened in Rue Quincampoix, and in the Marais, near Saint-Paul. It's obvious that this served only one purpose: to get rid of the poor who lived there and replace them with people who had the means to pay. We're well outside the framework of rehabilitation when we radically change usage and move in the direction of greater space, increased pleasure, the conquest of new qualities. Embalming is the opposite. We break up small apartments, cut the windows in two with new floors, et cetera. New York isn't exactly the same. There the industrial spaces were turned into dream apartments, unique spaces three hundred square meters in size. You can live in a building that's thirty meters deep. Once you have good lighting at either end, you can accept the fact that there are darker areas in the center, contrary to the hygienic theories favored by modernity. But what's happening in this case is more than a rehabilitation; it's also a mutation, and that mutation initiates a real shift in the way we understand a place aesthetically. In such spaces, a table, three chairs, and a bed are sufficient to create a poetics of space that differs from what it was when it was saturated with merchandise and machinery.

J.B. The modification you describe is an interesting approach to the situation. Can it be generalized? Could it politicized?

J.N. To politicize it, you would need to create an awareness on the part of "politicians." Can they understand and accept that every transformative act, every modification, is a cultural act as essential as creating something from scratch? Can they accept the fact that architecture is expressed and must increasingly be appreciated from within, a privileged space of enrichment, of nuance? . . . History provides us with beautiful examples of architectural forms that culminated in sedimentation, complementarity. The most convincing demonstration, a brilliant proof of the theory, may be the work of Carlo Scarpa. The first political question becomes: "What do I destroy? What do I preserve?" As a foil we have the memory of two grotesque periods of utter dreariness: the "destroy everything" period of the sixties and seventies, bulldozer renovation, followed by the "embalming" period—"Let's keep everything," let's create a pastiche, let's try to economize the architectural act.

Architectural Reason

J.B. Today things are designed for change; we have mobile, flexible, open-ended devices. We need to design an architecture based on computer logic, which is happening everywhere anyway. Then there's multiculturalism, the possibility of changing one's identity, of putting a number of computer avatars into play, which is supposedly an essential aspect of modernity, or transmodernity, I'm not quite sure.

I've been thinking a lot about this lately. There must be a difference between things that change and things that become. Yes, there's a fundamental difference between change and becoming. Things that "become" are rare, exposed to misunderstanding, and possibly disappearance. Becoming is not the same as importing change, initiating it, wanting it at any price, imposing an imperative of change on people—which is the credo of fashion, for example—from which they never escape. That's not necessarily how things become something. Can a city change before our eyes? Of course we can transform it, modify it, but does it "become" something, then? We can say that cities have "become" things over time. It's not a question of creating nostalgia, but cities, in the past, ended up acquiring a kind of singularity, while here, now, before our eyes, they change at top speed, in a state of confusion. We're watching their characteristics erode. Even modification may be a way of reintroducing things into the process of change, where they would have risked being either destroyed or purely and simply "museified," which is another miserable fate. Can we counteract change with another kind of need? Maybe we can go further: What will the city become?

J.N. Working on what a city will become implies having a heightened awareness of its identity and requires that we help direct change. Change is fatal, automatic, inevitable, and many of our leaders, including city mayors, demand change because it's a sign of vitality, a form of growth that can excuse a range of absurdities. What a city becomes is decided on the basis of what came before, not some hypothetical future designed by a long-term planning effort. What it will become provides opportunities for the expression of a contextual and conceptual architecture that is both anchored and enriching. Change for the sake of change provides all sorts of excuses for just about anything; in that sense, it's part of the lapse of architectural reason. It can come about through the automatic reproduction of market models, as well as from a conception of the future based on the cloning of preexisting buildings.

J.B. The lapse of architectural reason would be clone architecture.

J.N. The historical development of cities, their evolution, has always bothered architects. It's a strange paradox. Architects are constantly modifying the urban fabric, yet they resist its evolution. They generally reproduce the previous period. They want to continue to build the city that was, and every time the city changes, they say, "It's no longer a city, it's a suburb, it's shameful. . . ." The evolution of the city in the twentieth century is supposed to have resulted in violent upheaval. Yet we've witnessed an architectural caste that has clung to the twentieth-century city, the reconstruction of the European city; they still want to build streets and squares as they did before. . . . But they're streets and squares devoid of meaning.

The City of Tomorrow

J.B. Yes, but that's not cloning, if you look at what happens. . . .

J.N. It's a form of reproduction, duplication. Architects always stick to earlier forms used in the past; they're terrified of seeing the city move in ways they've worshiped, ways that they reproduced themselves. The evolution of the city—I'm being somewhat anticipatory—will continue to cause them anguish because a process of complete deterritorialization is taking place.

We are all urban. What characterizes a city today is a space shared by a certain number of people in a given period of time: the time it takes to get there, move around, meet other people. From the moment we—many of us—can access or share a territory, we belong to that territory, and that territory becomes urban. We belong to a city. We're going to end up urban even if we live in the country, on our little farm twenty kilometers from the nearest village. We will also be part of the "city." Time, not space, will determine our being a part of urban life in the future.

J.B. Only in the vision you've just given of the city to come, the city is no longer a form in the process of becoming; it's an extended network. That's fine, you can define it as you have, but that urban life is no longer the life of the city but its infinite possibility: a virtual urban life, like playing on the keyboard of the city as if it were a kind of screen. I saw it as the end of architecture . . . by pushing the concept to its limit and primarily by using the photograph as a point of departure. This is reflected in the idea that the great majority of images are no longer the expression of a subject, or the reality of an object, but almost exclusively the technical fulfillment of all its intrinsic possibilities. It's the photographic medium that does all the work. People think they're photographing a scene, but they're only technical operators of the device's infinite virtuality. The virtual is the device that wants nothing more than to function, that demands to function. And to exhaust all its possibilities. Doesn't the same thing happen in architecture, with its infinite potential, not only in terms of materials but in terms of models, all the forms that are available to architects (postmodern or modern)? From that moment on, everything is arranged according to . . . We can no longer even speak of truth, in the sense that there might be a finality to architecture, but we can't speak of radicality, either; we're in the realm of pure virtuality.

Virtual Architecture, Real Architecture

J.B. So is there still an architecture in the virtual sense? Would it still exist? Or should it exist? Can we continue to call it architecture? We can combine things, techniques, materials, configurations in space indefinitely, but will it produce architecture? I finally realized that the Guggenheim in Bilbao was typically the type of object made of complex compositions, a building established using elements whose modules are all exposed, all the combinations expressed. You could imagine a hundred museums of the same type, analogous, obviously none of which would resemble one another.

J.N. You can rely on Frank Gehry to surprise you!

J.B. He's wonderful—it really is marvelous—and I'm not making a value judgment about the object itself, but the structure of production and fabrication that made the building possible. As I see it, this architecture no longer possesses the literality I was talking about, that is, the presence of a singular form that couldn't be translated into another form. The Guggenheim itself is infinitely translatable into many other kinds of objects, as part of a chain. . . . You get the impression that there could be a possibility of architectural evolution in this way. But let's say, to go back to my photography example, that the camera itself generates a nearly uninterrupted stream of images. If we accept this, the device could reproduce everything, generate images endlessly. And within that visual stream we can hope that there are one or two exceptional images that don't obey this indefinite, exponential logic of technology. But isn't this similar to the risk architecture is exposed to? At bottom, since we were talking about readymades, I would say that the Guggenheim is a readymade. All the elements are there from the start. The only thing we need to do is transpose them, permute them, play with them in different ways, and we've made architecture. Only the transposition itself is automatic, a bit like an automatic writing of the world or the city would be. We can imagine whole cities built on this principle. . . . In some American cities, this is already true. And it's no longer just an engineering question. In the past we could say that engineers constructed, generation after generation, based on minimal standards. But in the Guggenheim example, something else is going on that starts with a creative model that is already virtual. We descend from virtuality to reality, in any event toward real existence—with the difference that, unlike information technology or mathematical modeling, in architecture, we end up with an object.

J.N. In the Bilbao Guggenheim, we're witnessing a new computer revolution in the service of architecture. That is, a new computer-based approach that would give substance to the idea, would lock or fix the most fleeting things, regardless of their immediacy. What's great about Frank Gehry is that he will make a sketch, crumple the paper, start over, and connect the sketch on paper or the relief drawing to an enormous program. From that point, the computer takes over and will begin to weave it all together, constructing an image in space, materializing something that is instantaneous and unstable, opening a direct passage from desire to the built reality. With Frank Gehry, we're watching this shortcut as it takes place, which is quite rare.

J.B. Even so, he has an extraordinary playing field to work with.

J.N. That's an optimistic assumption.

J.B. When you walk around the Guggenheim, you realize that the building is, as far as its lines are concerned, illogical. But when you see the interior spaces, they are almost completely conventional. In any case there is no relation between those spaces and the building's ideality.

J.N. Some of them are conventional because they have to obey museographical conventions. We haven't found a better way to exhibit Kandinsky, Picasso, and Braque other than on bright walls in quiet spaces. But there are also singular spaces: the lobby, the large hall, which is 250 meters long. Finally, there's also an attempt to adapt dream to reality, as always, but a very beautiful adaptation. . . . However, where I do see a danger—and I'm talking about 90 percent of global production at this time, certainly for all the large buildings—is in this way of making architecture by recycling existing computer-based data and coupling that with an extremely curtailed design procedure for the building. We're currently experiencing a wave of architectural cloning. From the moment an office building is made on the basis of an existing typology, whose technology and price and the conditions for its realization are known, we can duplicate that building and have it constructed without having to pay for a new design. This has resulted in the introduction of well-defined technical procedures that enable companies to enter the international market. In Asia, South America—look at São Paulo, for example—buildings are going up where there is no sense of architectural intent at all. It's a form of architectural sabotage, prostitution. You used film and the world of politics as examples, both of which are also undergoing wholesale sabotage. Well, here I see architectural sabotage. You get the impression that architects themselves are going to produce the types of buildings that totally counter anything that could result in quality or a sense of nobility for a city. This type of architecture is proliferating at an alarming rate. The most efficient economic models are moving in that direction. . . .

Computer Modeling and Architecture

J.N. Is there anything easier than reusing existing data, given the fact that the computer can modify that data so quickly? You change a parameter here, another there, and after a few hours, it's done. The system is ready for a new building. Consequently, buildings are not really thought out; they are based on immediate profitability and hasty decision making. This also involves the complete sacrifice of a dimension that many feel belongs to another time. . . . There is no further need for public spaces, no further need to compose; all we have to do is accumulate. I need to buy a building. This is the way I can have it for the lowest cost and as quickly as possible. The parameters are simple, there's no need for any equations.

J.B. Within that architectural space, does the possibility still exist for the architect to make his mark?

J.N. Most of the time there is no architect in the sense generally understood. There are engineers who are pretty efficient at working with the standards. And those standards are associated with certain humanist or behavioral attitudes. In Europe, for example, you can't sell an office building that doesn't have direct light. In the United States, for a variety of reasons, standards can differ considerably from those in Europe. For example, you're authorized to use artificial light. In other words, let's say you have a building that's fifty meters deep and your offices are in the center of the building; you'll see the first window twenty meters away, and you'll be in artificial light all the time. Those buildings, which are the cheapest to build, sell well in Asia and South America. But no consideration is given to human comfort. And it isn't the "developed" countries that have the most advanced humanist standards! Often it's in the poorest cities that you find spontaneous acts of creation. These can be considered magnificent architectural achievements, even when they use corrugated sheet metal or pieces of rag. Here we can identify a poetics that is really a form of creation, whereas in the other cases, we're getting pretty far away from that.

J.B. So what constitutes a particular space today, assuming architects still have any creative freedom?

J.N. Fortunately, all the conditions aren't in place yet for eliminating architecture. Within the evolution of the city there will always be a marginal place left for a handful of aesthetes—aesthetes in their own life and in their behavior—within highly privileged environments. What I wonder most about is what those cities will become. . . . In the near future, they won't be anything like what we're familiar with today. If the South is going to develop and catch up to the level of the cities of the North, using the same methods, it's going to take generations, and I don't see where the money is going to come from. No, I think there we're going to witness a true mutation.

Lightness and Heaviness

J.N. I even think that the next architectural and urban mutation will affect our relationship to matter. Other forms of mediation will be involved, and the mutation will shift toward the immaterial. Everything that is immaterial, virtual, sonorous, and part of the world of communication is already mutating. For example, anything that doesn't involve the creation of complex infrastructures will have an advantage. Everything that avoids pushing energy through enormous conduits, high-voltage lines, that sort of thing. Our thoughts for the future should be focused on autonomy, lightness. This will lead us to the promotion of emerging and environmentally friendly forms of energy such as solar or wind energy, satellite communications for the transmission of data, everything that fosters the local breakdown of waste rather than its centralization. It is this kind of thinking that can give rise to new strategies that will completely alter our current notion of urban development, an evolution that will result in the appearance of a "noncity" city, an urban territory. This kind of development can take into account the need for stable development. I'm describing a growing trend, and we're still a long way off from its realization, but it seems to me that this is one example of a realizable utopia.

J.B. Unfortunately I feel that in the future, as you mentioned, the great majority of construction, of building needs, will be technocratic, modeled. We will also have a luxury architecture reserved for a handful of privileged individuals. We see this happening in a number of fields, society, art . . . and the trend is toward increasing discrimination—contrary to what we believe—a discrimination that runs counter to the objectives of democracy and modernity. I'm not sure whether or not architecture can play a role in all this. Even so, it has wanted to play a role in these developments, an equalizing role, if not a humanist one.

J.N. Yes, but then this would be a result. Unfortunately it's not through architecture that we're going to change the world!

What Utopia?

J.B. Yes, that's true, but I'm an idealist, I still believe we can change the world through architecture. . . . It's utopian for all intents and purposes, yes. Utopian architecture was ultimately a realized architecture. But in the future, doesn't the trend risk moving in the opposite direction? Isn't there some danger that architecture may become a tool of discrimination?

J.N. Although architecture may be unable to influence politics to change the world, politics has a responsibility to make use of architecture to achieve its social, humanitarian, and economic objectives. The economic dimension of culture—whether it's architectural or not—is taken into account in the industrialized countries. Since I'm an idealist as well, I dream about programs for quickly resolving the living conditions of those who are most disadvantaged. But not using traditional poured-concrete solutions, which end up cloning monotonous seventies-style towers and linear block buildings in Seoul and São Paulo. No, I'm praying for genuine self-awareness. Only the readymades can provide very, very low production and distribution costs through automated production that can generate millions of copies. In today's shantytowns, it's easier to have a car or a television than a sink. . . . I dream of project requirements that incorporate the use of the least-expensive materials, the lightest, most flexible, easiest to cut and assemble, drill or handle. . . . corrugated tin, ribbed plastic, lightweight channel, cables, sheet metal, project requirements that include the hardware, small ready-made machines produced by the millions, which can make the best possible use of our knowledge of energy self-sufficiency. . . . I dream about habitat packages that can be parachuted in, along with a few tools, but don't predetermine the shape of the structures that can be built. I'd like to replace the old concept of the seventies of an architecture designed for the greatest number with an individual architecture not based on some cookie-cutter model. . . . I don't know of a single UNESCO program today that's pushing this in any radical way. Still, we're not heading for disaster; we're already in the midst of total disaster.

J.B. This year, in Buenos Aires, I spoke about the future of architecture. Yes, I believe in its future even though, as you mention, it won't necessarily be architectural, for the simple reason that we haven't yet designed the building to end all buildings, we haven't yet created the city to end all cities, a thought to end all thoughts. So as long as this utopia remains unrealized, there's hope, we must go on. We have to recognize that everything that's happening now on the technological side is dizzying, the modification of the species, and so forth. . . . However, in twenty years we will have succeeded in making the transition from sexuality without procreation to procreation without sexuality.

J.N. Let's change the mode of reproduction for architecture! Let's invent a sexual reproduction of architecture.

J.B. Procreation without sexuality challenges the idea of sexuality without procreation—which has been the essence of eroticism. As the laboratory grows in importance, the field of eroticism will, for the most part, start to implode. . . . But sexuality isn't the only thing. . . . With genetic engineering, they're in the process of studying genes for future modification. American clinics already exist where people can type in the characteristics of their future infant so that it doesn't turn out homosexual. . . . Obviously, most of it is a scam, but that doesn't matter because there is total belief in the fact that we'll be able to improve the species, that is, invent another species. If we look at the human species as it is, or architecture as a historical form, or the city as a symbolic form, what comes afterward? An exponential proliferation of things in combinatorial fashion? At that point, we've entered an abstract mental space, but one that's realized. They're not just formulas.

J.N. We can make an analogy. Imagine the cloning of genetically programmed buildings; it's easier with buildings than with people. It's a kind of new superfunctionalism, virtual functionalism, which is not the functionalism of the old organic and social functions, use value, et cetera. It's something different. We need to determine if the new data are going to remain significant, since we're currently witnessing the sacrifice of architecture. Perceptible data are becoming a thing of the past. We can be optimists and assume that we're going to become true virtuosos of this new programming and we'll be able to integrate a whole range of information and assumptions capable of producing an absolutely terrific space, articulated around the problematic of the environment that's been eating at us. It's a question of survival. We have to integrate modern ecology.

J.B. The environment, ecology . . . I'm prejudiced against them. I feel that ecology exists precisely through the disappearance of "natural" data. Everything that is part of nature or natural must be eliminated if we are to build a perfect artificial world, where natural species will exist in "artificially protected" reserves.

Architecture as the Desire for Omnipotence

J.B. You get the feeling that the desire for omnipotence that drives architecture—look at large government projects, for example—no longer has anything to do with the image of itself it wants to project, a bit like what's going on in genetic engineering. A geneticist today thinks he's replacing the mother and the father: he's the one who creates the child! He's the deus ex machina that creates the child, a child who originates with him and is no longer embedded in a sequence of natural descent.

J.N. It's been a long time since architects thought they were gods! Their only fear is that someone is going to snatch that dream away. Architecture is simply the art of necessity. Three-quarters of the time, aside from the necessity of use and custom, there is no architecture—or it's sculpture, commemoration.

J.B. There's a funny little museum—I'm sure you're familiar with it—that was built by Kenzo Tange in Nice. It's adorable. It's a delicious little building that sits on a body of water, not far from the airport. It was built about three or four years ago and has remained empty since then because there was never any funding to buy content for it. So the museum has remained empty, and it's marvelous, a jewel. Over the past five or six years, Kenzo Tange hasn't built anything himself. So this may be the last project he accepted. . . . He had reached his zenith.

J.N. Sometimes the name of a great architect is like a brand. So we continue to build under the Kenzo Tange brand. I'm in a very good position to know this because I discovered a bad clone of one of my projects in Tokyo. The basic project involved the grid of the horizon used for the Tête Défense, the perspective background for the historical axis between the Louvre and the Arc de Triomphe, a project that was awarded second prize in the president's competition in 1982. Sprekelsen won first prize for the Grande Arche, which is now completed.

My design was an attempt to go beyond traditional Albertian

perspective, where the sky is an always unfinished canvas. During the classical period, unfinished canvases revealed a checkerboard network of fine lines behind the painting that served as a grid so that the original cartoon could be enlarged. In my case, I imprinted a disembodied network on the horizon, dividing the void in the Arc de Triomphe into barely visible squares. The building was a three-dimensional orthogonal grid, like a gigantic Sol LeWitt sculpture. The sun set along the axis, directly to the west, to create what I call "mathematical sunsets." From a distance, it was two-dimensional, without depth; from up close it provided a sense of hyperperspective, a bit like an Escher drawing. So in Tokyo they built this three-dimensional grid and included, following the same proportions as La Défense, a building at each end. But since the building wasn't carefully situated with respect to the setting sun, they built an artificial sun into the grid, a ball of shiny steel that, in the evening, was artificially illuminated with red, violet, orange light.... When I saw the building one evening, from a distance, I thought I was hallucinating.... But as fate would have it—and you should enjoy this—the fatal element is that on the other side of Tokyo Bay, just a few kilometers away and separated only by the water, I was building a large, airy tower. From my project in Tokyo, I could see my grid, my mathematical sunset, and an artificial sunset!

J.B. And what about your projects for the Universal Exposition in Germany? We have a pretty good script about the work: the living work, the dead work, the spectral work. The spectral is self-perpetuating, like life; death is scattered among all the virtual productive forms. Some thought went into that project.

J.N. I explained that to Frédéric Flamand, the choreographer, who is going to stage this living spectacle like an exposition.... The big question that remains is the freedom of artists working with partnerships that only provide financing if they like the message.... This is no longer traditional sponsorship.... But that's the way exhibitions will be financed in the future. They will sponsor set design. . . . We're inside the subject. We'll have to provide subtitles.

Berlin and Europe

J.B. Does Berlin have any special meaning for you, as part of contemporary Europe?

J.N. Berlin's destiny is an intimate part of the century. It's a historic capital with a fabulous heritage—much of it due to K. F. Schinkel—that became capital of the Third Reich, was given the once-over by Speer, was partly destroyed, but survived, a captive abandoned to its conquerors. The city was martyred, cut up in pieces, and it still bears the stigmata. Then the city was freed and betrothed to Europe. . . . once again a queen. It's a great story, straight out of Dumas—the Countess of Monte Cristo!

J.B. And what about the center of the city? Is there any stated political or urban plan that's been expressly implemented?

J.N. The urban policy referred to as "critical reconstruction" goes something like this: "Let's pretend nothing ever happened. . . . Let's reconstruct traditional buildings, opaque walls and small windows. Let's triumphantly fill everything that's empty. Let's put the cupola back on the Reichstag." There had been some vague impulse to establish an urban strategy when the Wall came down. One of the major dailies organized an appeal for ideas directed to seven or eight international architects. I proposed to them that they transform the no-man's-land near the Wall into a long "meeting line," which would serve as a place where all the city's cultural events, sports, leisure activities, bars, restaurants, nightclubs, would be concentrated, face-to-face. By reversing the previous situation, the dividing line would become a weld, fullness would succeed the void, joy follow sadness, freedom prohibition. . . . But most of all, the city's history would remain embedded in its streets and stones. . . . I feel that the desire to wipe away those years is antithetical to the development of Berlin's identity and specificity. The city has plenty of reasons to be proud of its uniqueness, to demonstrate that it was able to make the most of a tragic past.

J.B. In Berlin there has been a temptation to historicize everything, to include even the most horrible things in the city's heritage. This reminds me of the time they thought one of Brazil's largest favelas was part of the world's patrimony.

J.N. Yes, before the fall of the Wall . . . But at the scale of the neighborhood, Berlin has shown a great deal of good sense in the way it has dealt with vegetation and water. The Germans are more fastidious than we are in working out microstrategies for innovation and management of the city on the day-to-day level.

J.B. Which is very different from Frankfurt and the other cities. Moreover, in 1968, when the same movements were under way in both Germany and France, there were more communities in Germany, but there were also larger apartments with common kitchens, and living was easier. In France we never succeeded; the big apartments were too expensive. By the way, it seems that the windows in the Galeries Lafayette . . .

Architecture as the Art of Constraint

J.N. Now, if the buildings are well-known, as soon as something happens, everyone knows about it. Still, you should be aware of the fact that the glass is designed to fall without injuring anyone. Like a car windshield. But I get the feeling that, in our age of hypersecurity, we're going to need more than safety glass! In fact, we've turned security into a key factor. Architecture is the art of constraint; we have to deal with that. I often use the example of film because we function much as movie directors—directors and architects are the ones who work with the most constraints in this cultural universe. We have roughly the same relationship to a client, or a producer, or a promoter. They give us a certain amount of money to work with, and they like to see it multiply, without having any disasters on their hands. We have crews that need to be directed within a given amount of time, and there's censorship. It's a very special situation, and ultimately quite different from anything a writer encounters.

J.B. If it's a question of security, then yes, it is.

J.N. The writer, the man of letters, the philosopher—they don't need to ask anyone's permission.

J.B. You seem to think that writing takes place without constraints. It's true that I have fewer than you, but as a writer, thinker, or researcher, I'm dependent on a system, for example, an editorial system, that is becoming increasingly incomprehensible.

J.N. The essential thing is that you, you can write a book that may be forgotten for thirty years if no one wants to publish your work, but it still exists, whereas a building in a drawing doesn't exist. . . . A manuscript, even when it's locked in a drawer, exists. A filmmaker who only writes treatments or an architect who only constructs drawings accomplishes nothing.

J.B. In that sense, the book is a prehistoric product! It's true that the book is not delivered to the reader or listener in real time, it only exists somewhere. But within a real-time hegemonic culture, the book exists for no more than a few weeks. That's the price we pay: it simply disappears.

J.N. There are miracles: Emily Dickinson was rediscovered many years later.

J.B. The science of security has total control. It's everywhere; it exercises control in the form of censorship. Health is also involved, all those so-called positive functions like protection, the environment. They can backfire dangerously by using censorship to fight singularity.

Transparency

J.B. Take the idea of transparency, for example. It's something extraordinary that expresses the play of light, with something that appears and disappears, but at the same time, you get the impression that it also involves a subtle form of censorship. This search for "transparency" with which our era is fascinated is at the very least ambivalent in its relation to power.

J.N. Obviously that's not exactly my ideological view of transparency! It's true that transparency can be awful if it is used incorrectly. What interests me in the evolution of architecture right now is the relation between matter and light, which can become something highly strategic. I'm much more interested in the relation between matter and light exposed by the transparency or opacity of glass, for example, than by formal spatial parameters. Throughout the century, we have explored a variety of techniques, and now we know just about where we are, and there's no apparent reason to choose one form rather than another. But the problem of "essence" (of a form, an architecture, a given space) is a much more contemporary problem, associated with the evolution of our knowledge about matter and quantum physics, the discovery of fractals, et cetera. These are the consequences of the advance science and technology have on our awareness of how we apprehend the world, space, time, which are also going to change our perceptual relation to space. The trend today is to consider that constructing a piece of architecture means becoming part of a continuum, it means building in space.

Light as Matter

J.N. You have to think of light as matter—and God knows, even for quantum physics, that's the crux of the problem. Physicists are currently trying to determine if a photon has mass, and they'll continue until they find its mass. For now, that mass is beyond what researchers are capable of determining, but they're pretty sure it exists. So what does "transparency" mean? If we use certain materials, we'll be able to program a building differentially over time and play with ephemeral effects. You could say that traditional or classic architecture has always played with the permanence of architectural effects. More and more, we're trying to work with concepts involving the programming of complex architectural effects for the same building. And working with transparency involves nothing more than working with matter to give a building different appearances. If I am working with glass, I can program what I'm going to see. It can depend on whether I light it from the front or the back; I can play with depth of field, with transparency in the strict sense of the term. I can work with backlighting and a number of other things. There's a way of treating transparency by interpreting it strictly: "I'm going to do something that won't be seen, and I'm going to see everything through it." On the architectural level, it's nothing but pornography. . . .

J.B. The opposite of a secret, obscenity.

J.N. My buildings try to play with the effects of virtuality, appearance. Viewers wonder if the material is present or not. We create virtual images, we create ambiguity. A building can play with transparency effects, but it does so through another element, which is reflection. At the Cartier Foundation building, the viewer never knows if they're seeing the sky or its reflection. Generally, you see both, and that ambiguity creates an interplay of multiple appearances. At the same time, the building makes use of the most trivial function of transparency for the exhibition space. There, you know that what is exposed in the interior is going to change the nature of the building, or at least one's perception of it—but it's designed for that. Walking in front of the building, you see a display.

J.B. That's what was so extraordinary about the opening of the Issey Miyake exhibit, because you had the designer's mobile elements inside, then you had a figurative representation formed by the guests themselves—most of the women were dressed in

Issey Miyake—which created a second element in the overall design. But you also made the entire building transparent, which served as the general set design. Standing outside the building, you saw the action unfold in the space where the items were displayed and which had itself become an object in the exhibition.

J.N. It would be very interesting to have a picture of the building that reveals all the exhibits that have taken place inside. One image I get a great deal of satisfaction from, in terms of understanding the Cartier Foundation space, is the *By Night* exhibition that took place there. The entire ground floor, plunged in darkness, remained completely dark for three months. That was part of the project. Transparency is also trans-appearance. . . . We shouldn't consider this an ideology based on our ability to reveal everything, control everything.

J.B. But that sense is still included in the idea of transparency, whether you want it to be or not. . . . And it implies a good deal more than just architecture. It implies all the means of information, a totality of information about oneself. . . . The idea of setting the attractions, the secrets of transparency against the dictatorship of transparency, of contrasting the interplay of the visible and the invisible against absolute visibility, is quite subtle. There are constructions that yield to the most trivial transparency, as a vector of power, focusing on the elimination of secrets. It only serves to reveal that it is no longer part of what we see.

Disappearance

J.N. What interests me about transparency is the idea of evaporation. Ever since man became man, he has fought against fate, against the elements, against matter. He started off building stone by stone, then made windows with small pieces of oiled paper, then learned how to do other things. There is a kind of architectural "Darwinism" at work, which is an evolutionary process through which man attempts to cover the maximum amount of space, the largest surface, insulate the most but with the least amount of material, without looking like he did anything. There's been a tremendous push forward that still isn't over and never will be. We can summarize it as follows: how can we resolve the most material problems with the greatest amount of elegance? It involves the domination of matter. For example, the progress made in glass technology during the century has been astonishing. Among other advantages, it's made from sand, and it doesn't require colossal amounts of energy. Glass has good durability, and now we are able to do more or less what we want with it. We can do a great job insulating glass because it contains particles that can't be seen with the naked eye. Glass can be opaque or transparent; it can change color. Glass is also a kind of language, a kind of mutant material, a material subject to a wide range of subtle treatments. Glass is a significant trend.

J.B. Isn't there a danger of seeing a proliferation of glass the way there was for plastic? A danger that it will become a universal material?

J.N. Yes, because it's very flexible in the way it can be used; you can do whatever you want with it. Because of this architectural Darwinism, glass has acquired a number of qualities; it lends itself well to the interplay of materials because it's the only material that allows you to visually program a building by giving it different looks. One of the trends in architecture today is to capture everything that can affect this awareness of the moment. We're also trying to capture variations of time, the seasons, the movements of visitors, and all of that is part of the architectural composition. There's also the idea of fragility, which is conveyed by the glass or by transparency—in the sense of a more living, more poignant reality. Even though, ever since banks started using glass for protection, transparency has taken quite a hit.

J.B. At least we still have the idea. In fact, like many others, the word "transparency" has undergone considerable semantic evolution. Previously it stood for a kind of absolute ideal. We could believe in the transparency of our social relationships or our relation to power. Now it's turning into a form of terror.

J.N. Yes, now it's become a pretext, and this didn't just begin today. Stained-glass windows were also used to similar effect. The Sainte-Chapelle was there long before we were! But if we consider that architecture involves creating a poetics of sorts, an instantaneous metaphysics, then transparency assumes a different meaning. You have the idea of the solid and the ephemeral. The concept of perennity still remains the characteristic of architecture that is most often acknowledged. Consider a pyramid. . . .

J.B. We want architecture to be something that survives us. However, that's no longer a factor for modern architecture—at least this is the way it seems to me. Or it's a factor that's been disguised, diverted; it's been turned into something like "saving time." Overtaking the moment.

J.N. Yes, but why is a building preserved? A building is preserved as soon as it's loved.

J.B. Humans, too!

What Does Architecture Bear Witness To?

J.N. When a building serves as a witness to a bygone era, it is preserved. If a building is considered a suitable prospect for bearing witness, even if it's very fragile, like Katsura or, an example closer to home, the Eiffel Tower or Beaubourg, it is preserved. The fact that we maintain it, spruce it up, repair it, preserve it in perfect condition, is part of a ritual of conservation. Once a building has reached this dimension of "bearing witness," it is, at least in a sense, archived, put under seal. Just because it's made of reinforced concrete or granite doesn't mean it will resist the depredations of time—the buildings constructed around the time of the Second World War are already in pretty bad shape, whatever Paul Virilio may think. In Berlin, for example, Bauhaus buildings have been preserved, while those from the fifties are being leveled left and right.

J.B. Le Corbusier's Villa Savoy has never been as lovely. It's been perfectly maintained and is more beautiful now than it was originally, more mature. I'd go as far as to say that our architectural heritage has been enriched. Look at the Oriental influence in Frank Lloyd Wright, wood and brick. Consider the destiny that would have had. . . . At the time, the avant-garde in architecture was involved with organic forms, made with ephemeral materials that weren't destined to last, like Las Vegas. For me, since I've known the city for thirty years, it's been a real massacre.

J.N. Sometimes the Americans are so outrageous that the result is really outstanding. We'll continue to complain about this outrageousness until the day we wake up in shock. . . . In any case, architecture is, paradoxically, unviewable; only a very small part of what's built counts. . . . Even Frank Lloyd Wright, who had considerable influence on the century, who built hundreds of houses, including Falling Water, a handful of large buildings such as the Johnson Wax building and the Guggenheim . . . Even with him, it's not so easy to uncover his tracks in the United States.

Singularity

J.N. Speaking of which, I very much liked what you said about our expectations of architects: that they are the ones still creating "singular objects."

J.B. I don't deserve the credit. . . . The object, in an unfortunate sense, is to an extent the end of architecture as something capable of translating a form belonging to the human community. Now, you mention "singular objects," which reflects a different quality of the object.

J.N. For more than twenty years, I've been defending the notion of the object's "hyperspecificity," contrary to all the typological, ideological, and dogmatic information that it comprises.

J.B. At some point, architecture is like poetry: you can provide all the interpretations of the poem you like, but it's always there. The object is literal in the sense that it is fully exhausted in itself.

You no longer wonder about architecture or poetry; you have an object that literally absorbs you, that is perfectly resolved in itself. That's my way of expressing singularity.... And it's essential that at a given point in time this singularity become an event; in other words, the object should be something that can't simply be interpreted, sociologically, politically, spatially, even aesthetically. The object may be quite beautiful and not be a singular object. It will be part of the general aesthetic, of global civilization. Yes, I think some can still be found.... But we also have to take into account the way the individual's singular perception divides the world. There are no standards, there are no formulas, there's no aesthetic or even functional matrix you can apply. The same object can satisfy all the functions we assign to it. That doesn't prevent it from possessing this extra quality.

J.N. Could we go so far as to say that the greater its singularity, the greater the chance it will be appreciated? That would be a consequence more than anything else.

J.B. Anything can be appreciated; I'm very skeptical about the notion.... It's not a question of relations, affects. You can have an affect for any object whatsoever that singularizes it for you. But at some point, what's needed is a different kind of awareness. If you like it, it becomes your dog and not someone else's. But this is something different, which is harder to articulate, because it can't be grasped intellectually.... It even seems to me that there's something a bit demoniacal in it, in the German sense of the word.

J.N. In the case of singularity, the aesthetics of the object is not fundamental to the extent that aesthetics obeys a type of convention, a type of judgment. You may feel an object is ugly, very ugly, uglier than ugly, monstrously ugly, and yet it can become in itself an entity that is absolutely essential. By that very fact, the object will become beautiful. Fortunately, it's not necessary to respect aesthetic codes to define singularity. The interesting thing is the ability to differentiate yourself from them and transgress them.

J.B. Take the Louvre Pyramid. At one point there was a movement to prevent its construction, because it was ugly. Then everyone calmed down.

J.N. It became widely accepted through use. But to me, it's not an example of a singular object.

J.B. It's obviously an academic object. But audacity, or the lack of audacity, is something that belongs not solely to an isolated object but also to the space it generates. At La Défense, in spite of everything, we can say that a strange space has been generated. Moreover, at first we don't know whether an object will become singular or not. This is what I referred to previously in terms of "becoming," of becoming—or not becoming—singular. It's a question not of change but of becoming. And this is something we can't determine. Sometimes even circumstances, whether they're historical, sociological, or whatever, trigger an object's singular becoming.

J.N. Pure event, "I perceive architecture as pure event," you said.

J.B. I'm interested in the things that shock me. I was writing about architecture as pure event, beyond beauty and ugliness.

J.N. But you contrast the "singular" with the "neutral" and the "global."

J.B. Yes, I differentiate global, universal, and singular.

J.N. And with respect to the neutral, you were kind enough to add: "We don't need architects for that!"

Neutrality, Universality, and Globalization

J.B. I would say the same for literature, thought, art, et cetera. Neutrality is assured; there's no problem with that. It's the total security we're offered day after day. Neutrality has never had a good reputation because neutral things are indifferent. At the very least, it signifies an absence of quality, the nonqualitative. It's not the kind of thing you can like; we perceive the mass, conformity. But now we're seeing the emergence of another form of neutrality, which appears in the literal sense of the term this time. In fact, all it can do is *appear*, since it is defined within a domain where all possibilities neutralize one another. This domain is different than before, when there was neither quality nor relief. Here it's the opposite. You have a "dynamic" neutrality that is open to so many possibilities that they are all neutralized, like the history of the still camera I mentioned earlier, a device that allows you to take all possible photographs. From that point on, you are neutralized as a subject. This neutrality, for me, is the baseline of the human species—and we can reach the same point in architecture, as well. It's a cultural effect, a choice, our choice. It's true, I contrast the singular with the neutral, but I also contrast it with the global. We need to be clear about our terms. There is a considerable difference between the universal and globalization. The universal remains a system of values, and in principle, everyone can access it. It's still the object of certain conquests. But little by little, it's becoming neutralized; cultures are being juxtaposed. Nonetheless the result is still a top-down equalization, through value, whereas in the process of globalization, we're witnessing a bottom-up leveling, according to the lowest common denominator. This is the "Disneyfication" of the world.

Unlike the values that drive universalization, globalization will be a theater of intense discrimination, the site of the worst discrimination. It will be a "pyramidal" globalization, so to speak. The society it generates will always be dissociated and no longer a society of conflict. One has the impression that between the two, that is, between those who will have access to information technology, the future "wired" world, and the others, the connection will have been broken. The two halves of society will become disconnected. They will each go down their own path, in parallel, and one will tend increasingly toward sophistication with respect to knowledge, speed, while the other will live with its exclusion—but without conflict, without any gateways. It's more dangerous than a revolt because it neutral-izes conflict itself. Forget about class struggle! There won't even be any "clashes." Forget revolution. There won't be any rela-tions of force; the fuse has melted. That's globalization. In the English-language press, the term refers primarily to economic markets. I mean something much more comprehensive. But it's the same underlying process if you look at it conceptually. It's an identification, a totalization—of the field of neutrality—it stands in contrast to the universal, which was an idea, a value, a utopia. This is the dimension of "realized" objects. In the case of the universal, it's the particular that stands opposite; in the case of globalization, it's singularity, a radicality of a different order. And one that doesn't enter into direct conflict with antagonis-tic forces. This isn't a revolutionary force; it exists elsewhere, is developed elsewhere, disappears. It's interesting to observe what remains of the irreducible in this process of globalization, this irreversible movement. This movement is a system, contrary to what the term would seem to imply, for the term "globaliza-tion" appears to imply that everything is comprised within it. But that's not the case. This movement is going to create a vir-tual hypersociety that will have access to all the resources—this much is clear—and all the power. Members of this hypersociety will be an absolute minority, an increasing minority, and in the majority of cases—in generic terms—the rest will remain excluded. So we'll be moving toward these parallel, dualistic societies, where things no longer function the same way on either side of the divide. What will that mean for life on earth? I don't know, but I have the impression that it's happening now in cities.

In this sense, the cities are prophetic. They are moving to-ward a kind of virtuality in terms of real, natural, traditional space. On the plane of the real, of reality, space is shared, while the most abstract virtual space is never shared. It's the privilege of those who have access to it. We won't be dealing with a domi-nant class any longer, but a computer-rich intelligentsia that will give free rein to complete speculation. Yet ultimately that's how Europe is being created. The euro, which is so much in the news today, is the epitome of the virtual object, imposed from above. All imposed decrees are established without any relation to actual opinion, but who cares, it will happen, and it did happen! Everyone will operate within a parallel market, a kind of black market, with its markups; everyone will organize their escape as well. Increasingly we'll see parallel sites spring up: parallel markets, parallel work, moonlighting, peripheral capitals, and so on. And in a sense, that's fortunate, because if control of one over the other were total, it would be an unbeatable defense strategy.

You almost get the impression that things were predestined to be this way.

Destiny and Becoming

J.B. For me, destiny is something that cannot be exchanged. This is true up to and including construction: what can't be exchanged for its own end is subject to destiny, to a form of becoming and singularity, a form of destiny. Predestination is a little different, for it claims that the end is already present in the beginning, but doesn't eliminate the end. In one sense, the end is already there; a cycle of predestination is then established. Destiny is what can't be inscribed within a finalizing continuity, something that can't be exchanged, whether for better or worse. I feel that thought, theory, is inexchangeable. It can't be exchanged either for truth or for reality. Exchange is impossible. It's because of this that theory even exists. However, there are many cases where exchange is possible. . . . Maybe this reflects the history of the city, architecture, space—there has to be a possibility of exchange so that things can be exchanged with one another. But sometimes they don't get exchanged at all. There may be no equivalent to a given building, there's no need, it can't be exchanged against anything else. They'll build another one, but as it stands, it can't be exchanged for something else. It's an unhappy fate, a failure in a certain sense. However, singular things can't be exchanged, either; they're autonomous. Only in this case, we can say that we're dealing with a fully realized form.

J.N. There's something that amused me in all this talk about destiny and fatality: when you finally advise the architect to not think!

J.B. Ah, yes! When I said that we have too many ideas. I say the same thing about philosophers, as well. . . . You have to differentiate thought from ideas. I don't recommend that they not think; I advise them against having too many ideas.

J.N. We know that this is difficult territory. We know our fate isn't clear to us, and yet we still need a minimum amount of strategy to deal with it. And that's what's actually going on. What kind of architecture can survive, what kind will still have meaning in tomorrow's world, in a context that we are in large part familiar with.

J.B. That we know almost too well. That's the problem.

The Idea of Architecture and History

J.B. One of the problems with today's architecture is that we can no longer make architecture without having an idea of architecture in mind, the history of architecture. In philosophy, for example, you have to take history into account, the references to which ideas are subjected by history, any number of heteroclite issues. That's where I say, "Let's not think too much!" Whenever you have an architectural project in mind, different data about space, history, the environment, the elements of the project, objectives, finalities, all of that provides you with the information to produce a disconcerting object that will be something quite different than the initial project. But if you project too much, if your conceptualization is too narrow, the lode runs out, and I think this is just as true in the field of theoretical research. People who accumulate every reference they can lay their hands on, multiplying the amount of data, carefully delineating the path they'll follow out toward infinity, exhaust themselves before they can say . . . what? Nothing.

J.N. Yes, we can make architecture that is not about architectural theory. Architecture is no longer an autonomous discipline. But that doesn't force us to think more, to broaden our field of investigation. The majority of the buildings in our cities weren't thought out in that sense. They arrived there through a kind of automatism, a lack of attention.... So I think, if we want singular objects, then we'll have to use various kinds of analysis, reflection, connotation; we'll have to establish relationships among contradictory objects. In short, we'll have to start thinking.

Another Kind of Wisdom

J.B. Look, I don't want to make a mystery of spontaneity. In fact, we should abdicate to serendipity.

J.N. Serendipity?

J.B. Serendipity, yes. In fact, no one knows the exact definition.... It's the idea of looking for something and finding something completely different.

J.N. But I'm a big fan of the sport! I've been practicing serendipity all my life without knowing it.

J.B. The important thing is to have looked. Even if you miss what you were initially looking for, the direction of the research itself shifts, and something else is discovered.... The concept is primarily applied to the sciences, but it's also the name of a store in London, where you can find all sorts of things, except whatever it is you're looking for. The word comes from the Sanskrit. It's a beautiful way of saying "wisdom." It has been anchored in sacred Indian literature for centuries.

J.N. At bottom we're looking for something, but we never know what. When we find it, everything is all right.... Fortunately, in architecture there's never a single correct response. There are millions of pathetic and a few thousand exciting responses. All we need is to find one that can be realized. But these responses are rarely simplistic. Paradoxically they are trying to be obvious but indecipherable. There's nothing worse than a building whose recipes we know by heart. In architectural conferences, you often hear people discuss kitchen recipes that result in the creation of a building. People don't always want to tell you "how," they don't want to reveal their strategy, but rather want to create an aura of mystery that's essential for a certain type of seduction.

The Question of Style

J.B. In Buenos Aires the presentation of buildings by different architects, all of them well-known, lasted five days. There was never a question of the mystery you speak of, only the nature of the projects, the development of a program, the results obtained, the international career of the person exposing his or her work. With respect to this sense of mystery, what we saw was incredibly impoverished.

J.N. We are dealing with thickness, something that will never be totally elucidated, deciphered. There will always have to be things that remain unsaid and things in which we lose ourselves. At the same time, an architectural work should be capable of being experienced by people with very different sensibilities. So we have to set up a certain number of markers that can capture the attention or the interest of this highly diverse group.

J.B. In a number of fields, this kind of sociological calculation is barely functional. The entire field of advertising is focused on this type of approach, but in reality they have no idea what they're doing.

J.N. It's true of literature, painting, music. The great works, the great books, are universal. They affect people from all cultures and all levels of education.

J.B. Yes, but to the extent that these artists are able to create without giving in to the farce of art, art history, or aesthetic codes. So it's possible, ultimately. It's as if the architect were able to build without first reviewing the field of architecture, its history, and everything that is constructed. The ability to create a vacuum is undoubtedly the prerequisite for any act of authentic creation. If you don't create a vacuum, you'll never achieve singularity. You may produce remarkable things, but the heritage you have to deal with is such that you'll have to pass through a whole genetics of accumulation.

J.N. Yes, but that doesn't rule out a strategy to flush out . . .

J.B. Architecture can't be as spontaneous as writing.

J.N. Certainly. Still, what characterizes architecture is its writing, the fact that we are able to recognize any detail at all. This doesn't only involve an exterior shape. And if you look at all the great architects of this century—Wright, Le Corbusier, Aalto, Kahn—you can recognize them by the details. This singularity of their architecture is remarkable. There must be something natural and spontaneous in it, but at the same time, it's planned, worked on, premeditated.

J.B. You could say predestined.

J.N. This activity of premeditation is the thing architecture needs the most at this time. It will prevent its banality, mindless repetition, autism.

J.B. Not just anyone has the means to make his mark on a building, but anyone can write a bad article. Facility, in this case, is dangerous.

J.N. No, but many people are under the illusion that depth, thought, comes about through omnipresent decoration. Decoration is used to palliate this absence of intent, the incoherence of architecture. Generally the architecture is hidden behind an ersatz facade. It's the obsession that makes the difference; with decoration you can mimic anything, any universe. There are decorators who could be considered architects. They work at revealing the spirit of the place. This was true during the thirties, and it's still true today when people like Starck succeed in transforming a place.

J.B. Do they still speak of style in architecture? Because compared to singularity, I would like to know what style is. . . . We recognize someone who has style, but the work produced won't necessarily be the embodiment of a singular vision.

J.N. Except if the style happens to be a singular vision. . . . It's one of the big questions in architecture. Style addresses the problem of the evolution of architecture. We can say that architects, in the twentieth century, have positioned themselves as artists in the plastic arts. They've appropriated the field; they've pretended it was also their own. Once this formal identification was made, the number of caricatures began to multiply: the ones who made everything white or everything blue, all in garlands, and so on. That's how myths get started. For example, historically Meier's architecture always turns out white. You're familiar with Ungers, who only does squares; Baselitz, the artist, turns things upside down. Those are perfectly identifiable styles that conceive of architecture as a preexisting vocabulary that can be used according to a preexisting code. A style, in my sense of the term, is something different. Style is a way of doing. But I can also suggest another definition. . . . Personally, I'm very interested in the way a style works, which has presented a problem—concerning me—for certain critics or certain individuals, who wondered, "What's this guy doing?" When an architect's way of doing something is identified, the way we recognize his style is as well. If these artist-architects build, their building will always be particular, since it will become their signature, in a way; but their approach has no relation to other particularities that they could exploit but don't. They are enclosed within a system. Style should reflect a singular way of thinking the world.

Inadmissible Complicity

J.N. You've said that you prefer complicity to complexity. I like the idea very much. It reflects a real problem in architecture. We manage to make things that are profound only through complicity, and perhaps only through this complicity do we achieve a certain degree of complexity, which isn't an end in itself. Often things are complex when they have to be, quite simply. This preliminary search for complexity has long been associated with a theory that claims that interesting things have to be complex because we then escape from a completely repetitive form of simplicity. The idea of complicity in architecture is more unusual, more uncommon. Complicity is the only guarantee that we'll be able to push the boundaries. But we need to consider this in a very broad sense. If this complicity is established, it means that something more than simple comprehension is going on between people, a shared meaning, mutual assistance. Obviously, I can't build the Cartier Foundation building if I don't establish a relationship of complicity with the person who conceived and manages it. And this complicity has to exist among the crew, an enterprise, a global project. There has to be a shared dynamic, one that's often unspoken but translated into actions. However, the word "complicity" is not always well received. In this world, where everyone is trying to find their place, if you start weaving privileged links, you're accused of plotting, of cheating. If you set up relationships that are more than contractual, if you begin to enjoy doing something, you're called on the carpet. . . . You're not supposed to have fun while doing architecture! And you're especially not supposed to talk about desire before talking about the project requirements. However, all the great architects made their careers by exploiting this sense of complicity between contractor and client. For example, look at Gaudi or Gehry: contractor and client were inseparable.

Freedom as Self-Realization

J.B. Like seduction, "complicity" is a term with a bad reputation. Both are contrasted with an ideology of transparency. The complicity of a connection can't be "exposed," but at best suggested. Personally, I'm not sure how free we are to accept such complicity. Obviously I have a kind of prejudice against freedom. Against liberation, in any case. Freedom has become the ideal of modernity. And this no longer seems to pose any problems. When the individual is freed, he no longer knows what he is. Be yourself! Be free! That's part of the idea, the new diktat of modernity. Under the constraints of this new liberation, the individual is forced to find an identity for himself. Today we still live with the ultimatum that we find our identity, fulfill ourselves, realize our full potential. In this sense we are "free" because we have the technical means for this realization. But this is a prodigal freedom and culminates in individualism. It hasn't always been like this. The freedom of a subject struggling with his freedom is something else. Today we have an individual who isn't struggling with anything but who has set himself the goal of realizing himself in every possible dimension. We can't really postulate the problem of freedom. It's no more than a kind of operationality.

J.N. Is that what you mean when you write, "Ultimately, we exist in a society where the concept of architecture is no longer possible, the architect no longer has any freedom"?

J.B. No, not exactly. What would freedom mean within an ideological field that is no longer the same? Freedom in a state of subjection, want, is an idea and, at the same time, a kind of destiny: you desire it, you look for it. Liberation is not at all the same thing as freedom. That's what I wanted to make clear. When you're free, when you think you're living a realized freedom, it's a trap. You are standing before a mirage of the realization of various possibilities. . . . Everything that was once idea, dream, utopia, is virtually realized. You are faced with the paradox of a freedom that has no finality. It's simply the consecration of your identity.

J.N. What are you saying?

J.B. Well, that you have the right to fulfill yourself in the name of this freedom. Simply put, at some point in time, you no longer know who you are. It's a surgical operation. The history of your identity helps set the trap. The sexes find their sexual identity, and nothing more is shared between them, they exist in their own bubble. Alterity? Freedom is charged with a heavy load of remorse. And the liberation of people, in the historical sense of the term, is also a fantastic deception. There is always an element of the unthinkable that won't have been evacuated. So there's a kind of remorse because of what's transpired. We're free—so what? Everything begins at the point where, in reality, we have the impression that something was supposed to be fulfilled. Take the idea that the individual becomes free—every man for himself, of course. At that point there is a terrible betrayal toward . . . something like the species, I don't know what else to say about it. Everyone dreams of individual emancipation, and yet there remains a kind of collective remorse about it. This surfaces in the form of self-hatred, deadly experimentation, fratricidal warfare . . . a morbid state of affairs. There is even a final requirement that this state of affairs itself be questioned. Liberation is too good to be true. So you look for a destiny, an alterity, which is artificial, most of the time. You're forced to invent the alterity, to invent something risky, to rediscover at least a kind of ideal freedom, not a realized form, because that really is unbearable. The absence of destiny is itself a fatality! So what can the architect do with this freedom?

J.N. The architect is not free himself. . . . And men are not free with respect to architecture. Architecture is always a response to a question that wasn't asked. Most of the time, we are asked to handle contingencies, and if while handling these needs, we can create a bit of architecture, so much the better. . . . But we also realize that three-quarters of the planet is not actively thinking about architecture. And where it is too present, people resent it. Where is the point of balance between these two extremes?

J.B. It's not a handicap; it's a strategic value.

J.N. Regardless of the future form our civilization takes, there will always be a place for architecture, there will always be a particular strategy for inhabiting it, a territory to defend. Even if we start with the assumption that the city will disappear, in the sense that it will no longer be physically present as a territory—which doesn't lend itself to an urban vision of architecture—there will still always be architectural acts that assume some relation to the new data and which will be a source of pleasure. We've been told that the book would disappear with the Internet, but we'll always need a home, some place to live. . . . Even if the architectural gesture tends to become increasingly automatic.

J.B. For cloned encephalons!

J.N. An automatic architecture created by interchangeable architects. This fatality doesn't bother us; it's an essential part of today's reality. We still have the exception to invalidate the rule.

The philosopher and writer **Jean Baudrillard** has taught at several universities around the world. He is the author of numerous books and essays. In English his most notable works are *Simulacra and Simulation, America, The Vital Illusion, Symbolic Exchange and Death,* and *Consumer Society.*

Jean Nouvel, an architect of international renown, has designed L'Institut du Monde Arabe and the Cartier Foundation in Paris. With Paul Jodard, he is author of *International Design Yearbook* (1995) and *Present and Futures: Architecture in Cities.* He also worked with Conway Lloyd Morgan on *Jean Nouvel: The Elements of Architecture.*

Robert Bononno is a recent recipient of a National Endowment for the Arts award for the translation of *Isabelle Eberhardt, Seven Years in the Life of a Woman: Letters and Journals.* His many translations include *Cyberculture* (Minnesota, 2001), *Kubrick: The Definitive Edition, French New Wave,* and *Ghost Image.*

K. Michael Hays is Eliot Noyes Professor of Architecture Theory at Harvard University and adjunct curator of architecture at the Whitney Museum of American Art. His publications include *Architectural Theory since 1968.*